Weapons of
Mass Destruction

O P P O S I N G   V I E W P O I N T S®

OTHER BOOKS OF RELATED INTEREST

OPPOSING VIEWPOINTS SERIES

American Foreign Policy
America's Defense
The Breakup of the Soviet Union
Eastern Europe
Islam
The New World Order
The Third World

CURRENT CONTROVERSIES SERIES

Interventionism
Nationalism and Ethnic Conflict
Urban Terrorism

AT ISSUE SERIES

Ethnic Conflict
The United Nations

2

Weapons of
Mass Destruction

O P P O S I N G   V I E W P O I N T S®

Jennifer A. Hurley, *Book Editor*

David L. Bender, *Publisher*
Bruno Leone, *Executive Editor*
Bonnie Szumski, *Editorial Director*
David M. Haugen, *Managing Editor*

OPPOSING
VIEWPOINTS®
SERIES

Greenhaven Press, Inc., San Diego, California

Cover photo: Artville, Image Club

Library of Congress Cataloging-in-Publication Data

Weapons of mass destruction / Jennifer A. Hurley, book editor.
      p.   cm. — (Opposing viewpoints series)
   Includes bibliographical references and index.
   ISBN 0-7377-0058-0 (pbk. : alk. paper). —
ISBN 0-7377-0059-9 (lib. : alk. paper)
   1. Weapons of mass destruction. 2. Nuclear terrorism. 3. Nuclear
weapons—United States. 4. National security—United States. 5.
United States—Defenses. I. Hurley, Jennifer A. II. Series: Opposing
viewpoints series (Unnumbered)
U793.W43 1999
358'.3—dc21   98-43910
                                                                      CIP

Greenhaven Press, Inc., P.O. Box 289009
San Diego, CA 92198-9009

 AUG - - 2002

"CONGRESS SHALL MAKE NO LAW...ABRIDGING THE FREEDOM OF SPEECH, OR OF THE PRESS."

First Amendment to the U.S. Constitution

The basic foundation of our democracy is the First Amendment guarantee of freedom of expression. The Opposing Viewpoints Series is dedicated to the concept of this basic freedom and the idea that it is more important to practice it than to enshrine it.

CONTENTS

WHY CONSIDER
OPPOSING VIEWPOINTS?

"The only way in which a human being can make some
approach to knowing the whole of a subject is by hearing
what can be said about it by persons of every variety of
opinion and studying all modes in which it can be looked
at by every character of mind. No wise man ever acquired
his wisdom in any mode but this."

John Stuart Mill

In our media-intensive culture it is not difficult to find differing
opinions. Thousands of newspapers and magazines and dozens
of radio and television talk shows resound with differing points
of view. The difficulty lies in deciding which opinion to agree
with and which "experts" seem the most credible. The more in-
undated we become with differing opinions and claims, the
more essential it is to hone critical reading and thinking skills to
evaluate these ideas. Opposing Viewpoints books address this
problem directly by presenting stimulating debates that can be
used to enhance and teach these skills. The varied opinions contained in each book examine many different aspects of a single
issue. While examining these conveniently edited opposing
views, readers can develop critical thinking skills such as the
ability to compare and contrast authors' credibility, facts, argu-
mentation styles, use of persuasive techniques, and other stylis-
tic tools. In short, the Opposing Viewpoints Series is an ideal
way to attain the higher-level thinking and reading skills so essential in a culture of diverse and contradictory opinions.

In addition to providing a tool for critical thinking, Opposing
Viewpoints books challenge readers to question their own
strongly held opinions and assumptions. Most people form their
opinions on the basis of upbringing, peer pressure, and personal, cultural, or professional bias. By reading carefully bal-
anced opposing views, readers must directly confront new ideas
as well as the opinions of those with whom they disagree. This
is not to simplistically argue that everyone who reads opposing
views will—or should—change his or her opinion. Instead, the
series enhances readers' understanding of their own views by
encouraging confrontation with opposing ideas. Careful examination of others' views can lead to the readers' understanding of
the logical inconsistencies in their own opinions, perspective on

why they hold an opinion, and the consideration of the possibility that their opinion requires further evaluation.

EVALUATING OTHER OPINIONS

To ensure that this type of examination occurs, Opposing Viewpoints books present all types of opinions. Prominent spokespeople on different sides of each issue as well as well-known professionals from many disciplines challenge the reader. An additional goal of the series is to provide a forum for other, less known, or even unpopular viewpoints. The opinion of an ordinary person who has had to make the decision to cut off life support from a terminally ill relative, for example, may be just as valuable and provide just as much insight as a medical ethicist's professional opinion. The editors have two additional purposes in including these less known views. One, the editors encourage readers to respect others' opinions—even when not enhanced by professional credibility. It is only by reading or listening to and objectively evaluating others' ideas that one can determine whether they are worthy of consideration. Two, the inclusion of such viewpoints encourages the important critical thinking skill of objectively evaluating an author's credentials and bias. This evaluation will illuminate an author's reasons for taking a particular stance on an issue and will aid in readers' evaluation of the author's ideas.

As series editors of the Opposing Viewpoints Series, it is our hope that these books will give readers a deeper understanding of the issues debated and an appreciation of the complexity of even seemingly simple issues when good and honest people disagree. This awareness is particularly important in a democratic society such as ours in which people enter into public debate to determine the common good. Those with whom one disagrees should not be regarded as enemies but rather as people whose views deserve careful examination and may shed light on one's own.

Thomas Jefferson once said that "difference of opinion leads to inquiry, and inquiry to truth." Jefferson, a broadly educated man, argued that "if a nation expects to be ignorant and free . . . it expects what never was and never will be." As individuals and as a nation, it is imperative that we consider the opinions of others and examine them with skill and discernment. The Opposing Viewpoints Series is intended to help readers achieve this goal.

David L. Bender & Bruno Leone,
Series Editors

Greenhaven Press anthologies primarily consist of previously published material taken from a variety of sources, including periodicals, books, scholarly journals, newspapers, government documents, and position papers from private and public organizations. These original sources are often edited for length and to ensure their accessibility for a young adult audience. The anthology editors also change the original titles of these works in order to clearly present the main thesis of each viewpoint and to explicitly indicate the opinion presented in the viewpoint. These alterations are made in consideration of both the reading and comprehension levels of a young adult audience. Every effort is made to ensure that Greenhaven Press accurately reflects the original intent of the authors included in this anthology.

INTRODUCTION

"The occasional leakages of fissile material [from Russian nuclear weapons facilities] involve such miniscule amounts—in fractions of grams, not the kilograms necessary—that building nuclear weapons is not technologically possible."

—William C. Martel

"It's a matter of 'when, rather than if' nuclear or biological warfare material will find its way from a poorly guarded Russian research laboratory, for example, into the hands of outlaw nations, drug cartels or extremist groups."

—Russell Shaw

The term "weapons of mass destruction" refers to weapons whose destructive capacity far surpasses that of guns or even conventional explosives. This category includes nuclear, chemical, and biological weapons. Nuclear weapons, considered by many to be the most deadly instruments of war ever devised, are highly explosive bombs whose energy comes from the fission of radioactive material. Chemical weapons, initially developed by the Nazis during World War II, are substances that kill through inhalation or contact with the skin. Biological warfare entails the intentional dissemination of lethal bacteria and viruses. What unites nuclear, chemical, and biological weapons is their potential to wipe out entire populations. World conflicts that involve weapons of mass destruction could lead to widespread annihilation, even apocalypse.

Some maintain that as more and more countries gain access to weapons of mass destruction, the use of these weapons is increasingly probable. Of greatest concern, say those who feel an apocalypse is likely, is the possession of weapons of mass destruction by "rogue" nations—countries that are considered unstable or hostile. According to some commentators, recent incidents suggest that rogue nations are not hesitant to develop and use highly destructive weapons: In the spring of 1998, India and Pakistan conducted underground tests of nuclear bombs, while North Korea developed a new ballistic missile capable of delivering nuclear, biological, or chemical weapons; moreover, evidence suggests that Iraq used nerve gas against its enemies during the Iran-Iraq War and the Gulf War. It is said that as nations in the Middle East and other volatile areas bolster their weapons capabilities, skirmishes have the potential to bring about disaster.

Furthermore, a number of analysts maintain that the disintegration of the former Soviet Union has increased the likelihood of terrorism involving weapons of mass destruction. According to these analysts, the disorganization and widespread unemployment resulting from the Soviet Union's collapse has created conditions in which terrorists can easily obtain dangerous weapons—either by stealing from unguarded Russian weapons facilities or by purchasing materials or information from the vast number of unemployed Russian weapons developers. Experts also insist that the Russian government contributes to weapons proliferation. Stephen Blank, professor at the Strategic Studies Institute at the U.S. Army War College, states that "Russia has become a conscious, willing, and major proliferator of weapons of mass destruction, including biological warfare capabilities." Furthermore, notes Blank, "Russia is . . . offering nuclear technology, weapons technology, and reactors to India, China, Pakistan, Cuba, Syria, Iraq, and Iran."

However, others argue that the proliferation of weapons of mass destruction and the ease by which these weapons are constructed is highly exaggerated. With regard to nuclear proliferation, Henry S. Rowen, former Assistant Secretary of Defense, states that "perhaps the most striking fact about the role of nuclear weapons . . . is how few countries that are able to make nuclear weapons have actually done so." According to Rowen and others, the fact that only nine nations—the United States, Britain, France, Israel, the Soviet Union, China, India, Pakistan, and South Africa—have developed nuclear capabilities suggests that the problem of nuclear proliferation is overstated.

Moreover, maintain those who discredit apocalypse theories, the notion that weapons of mass destruction are widely available is a myth. In fact, some experts argue, the materials and technological knowledge needed to construct such weapons is extremely difficult to obtain. In the case of chemical or biological weapons, potential antagonists face a variety of obstacles: Deadly substances are hard to find, dangerous to handle, and nearly impossible to spread. As for the threat of a nuclear attack, some observers point out that although nuclear weapons have existed for over five decades, neither terrorists nor nations have ever used these weapons, excepting the United States. Joseph F. Pilat, who writes frequently on the subject of nonproliferation, notes the tendency of many commentators to "hype the threat of nuclear, biological, and chemical . . . terrorism."

Although disagreement prevails over the likelihood of apoca-lypse, both sides agree that policies related to weapons of mass destruction must be devised with care. *Weapons of Mass Destruction: Opposing Viewpoints* spotlights the controversy over weapons policy in the following chapters: How Likely Is a Terrorist Attack Involving Weapons of Mass Destruction? What Policies Should the United States Adopt Toward Nuclear Weapons? How Can the United States Defend Itself from an Attack? Will International Treaties Curb Weapons Proliferation?

CHAPTER 1

HOW LIKELY IS A TERRORIST ATTACK INVOLVING WEAPONS OF MASS DESTRUCTION?

CHAPTER PREFACE

At the height of morning rush hour on March 20, 1995, terrorists stationed on the trains of three Tokyo subway lines used umbrella tips to puncture plastic bags filled with sarin gas—a deadly chemical developed by the Nazis during World War II. As the gas dispersed, thousands of passengers staggered out onto the street, some with headaches and chest pains, others bleeding from the nose or vomiting uncontrollably. The attack, which left twelve people dead and over 5,000 injured, was attributed to the fanatical Buddhist cult Aum Shinrikyo.

Some commentators claim that the Aum Shinrikyo attack has wide-reaching implications about the likelihood of chemical or biological terrorism. According to Jonathan B. Tucker, the Director for Chemical and Biological Weapons Proliferation Issues at the Center for Nonproliferation Studies, "As the first large-scale terrorist incident involving a lethal chemical agent, [the Tokyo subway attack] weakened a longstanding psychological taboo and raised the spectre of more such incidents in the future." Tucker and other analysts view the attack as clear evidence that terrorists have the capacity to create chemical or biological weapons—and the inclination to use them.

Others regard the Aum Shinrikyo attack as an isolated event that does not foretell future acts of chemical or biological terrorism. If anything, some commentators argue, the incident proves how difficult chemical or biological terrorism is to plan and execute: Despite the fact that Aum Shinrikyo is highly organized, technologically savvy, and possesses an estimated $1 billion in assets, the cult was still unable to launch an attack that produced mass casualties. Moreover, maintain a number of weapons experts, chemical and biological weapons are not the ideal tools for terrorism because they are difficult to disperse and are less predictable than conventional explosives. Physical chemist Graham S. Pearson notes that "there is . . . the real risk that the terrorists may harm themselves through their mishandling of [chemical or biological] materials."

The controversy over the implications of the Aum Shinrikyo sarin gas attack reflects a larger debate about the likelihood of terrorism involving weapons of mass destruction. The chapter that follows provides contrasting perspectives on whether chemical, biological, or nuclear terrorism is an impending threat.

"The more likely threat to our
national security is not a nuclear
war but attacks by terrorists using
small amounts of [chemical or
biological] agents to cause numerous
casualties."

CHEMICAL AND BIOLOGICAL
TERRORISM IS A SERIOUS THREAT

Vinod Jain and Bharati Dhruva

Chemical and biological (CB) weapons are harmful substances
that can cause widespread death or disease if released in a populated area. In the following viewpoint, Vinod Jain and Bharati
Dhruva contend that CB weapons in the hands of terrorists constitute a serious threat to U.S. security. According to the authors,
terrorists may favor CB weapons because they are inexpensive to
produce, highly toxic, and extremely difficult to detect. Jain is a
technology analyst with a consulting firm in Virginia. Dhruva is
a research associate at Johns Hopkins University specializing in
biotechnology.

As you read, consider the following questions:

1. According to Leonard Cole, what are some possible scenarios
   of CB terrorism?
2. In what ways is the U.S. government preparing for CB
   terrorism, according to Jain and Dhruva?
3. What are the stages of response to a CB attack, in the authors'
   words?

Abridged from Vinod Jain and Bharati Dhruva, "Agents of Terror." This article appeared
in the November 1997 issue of, and is reprinted with permission from, The World and I, a
publication of The Washington Times Corporation; copyright ©1997.

With the end of the Cold War, the United States stands as the world's single, undisputed superpower. Until then, the most serious concern about this nation's security was the possibility of a nuclear showdown with the Soviet Union. Now, however, the threat of a nuclear attack on U.S. soil has considerably diminished. In its place, a new menace looms over our civilian population: terrorist activity employing chemical agents or biological pathogens.

Over the past few decades, while terrorist activities have risen, they have generally been carried out with common firearms or explosives. Our antiterrorism measures, therefore, have involved detecting weapons of this nature. Chemical and biological (CB) weapons, on the other hand, have been regarded by most Americans as too remote and esoteric to have much relevance to our daily lives.

In fact, toxic industrial chemicals—chlorine and phosgene—were used in World War I, and Nazi Germany converted insecticides for military use in World War II. More recently, Iraq used chemical weapons in its war against Iran and then threatened to use them against UN troops during the 1991 Gulf War. Those were open acts of war. But a new threshold was crossed in March 1995, when a Japanese terrorist group surreptitiously released the chemical agent sarin in a Tokyo subway train, killing 12 people and injuring about 5,500. Many more people would have died if the sample of sarin had been of higher purity. Several copycat incidents followed.

A WAKE-UP CALL

The Tokyo incident was a wake-up call, demonstrating the viability of CB weapons as agents of terror. It served to confirm that terrorist groups can both acquire and use such weapons to injure or kill large numbers of people. And it exposed the vulnerability of even a technologically advanced nation to terrorism of this nature. This incident raised an important question in the minds of many in the U.S. Congress and among health, safety, and law-enforcement officials here: Are Washington, D.C., and other major metropolitan areas safe from a terrorist attack employing such weapons?

The growing fear is that CB agents in the hands of a well-trained terrorist organization, whether state-sponsored or stateless, would be a lot deadlier than if employed by a lone amateur. Partly because of such possibilities, many experts now believe that the more likely threat to our national security is not a nuclear war but attacks by terrorists using small amounts of CB agents to cause numerous casualties. Sen. Richard Lugar (R-Indiana) echoed this when he said that "terrorism involving weapons of mass destruction is one of our most urgent national security priorities."

ASSESSING THE THREAT

Experts who have studied the potential of CB terrorism agree that the threat is both real and serious. Reflecting this concern, Kyle Olson, past executive vice president of the Chemical and Biological Arms Control Institute, based in Alexandria, Virginia, has been quoted as saying, "It is not a question of 'if'; it is a question of 'when.'" The danger is compounded by the assessment that most U.S. cities are not appropriately prepared to deal with it. In 1996, former CIA Director John Deutch testified before Congress that the United States is poorly organized and inadequately equipped to defend itself against a terrorist group armed with nuclear, biological, or chemical weapons.

Why should the public be more worried about terrorists using CB agents than other weapons? Among the most significant reasons are the degree of lethality of CB agents and the psychological impact they have. For instance, the nerve agent sarin can kill a person within minutes after contact or inhalation. A purified form of botulin, a biological toxin that causes botulism, is roughly three million times more potent than sarin, according to a report of the former Congressional Office of Technology Assessment.

In his book *The Eleventh Plague: The Politics of Biological and Chemical Warfare*, author Leonard Cole writes that the possible scenarios are "endless." One example he gives is the contamination of a city's water purification system by biological agents. A small amount of botulin in the water system could theoretically kill millions, says Cole. He also details past tests by the U.S. Army in a number of scenarios. These included spraying San Francisco with bacteria from an offshore boat, tossing lightbulbs filled with bacteria on New York City subway tracks, and spreading chemicals with fans from perforated suitcases in a Washington, D.C., bus station. The materials used in these tests were relatively harmless, but they aided in assessing the potential damage from CB weapons.

For the would-be terrorist, CB agents offer several advantages. They are comparatively cheap to produce, requiring just a small laboratory or facility. Some are industrial or research materials that may be obtained through legitimate channels. In addition, they are easily deployable—they may be left in a small, unattended package, for example. They are harder to detect than explosives and firearms, which can be revealed by various instruments such as metal detectors and X-ray machines. And small quantities of CB agents are sufficient to cause widespread harm.

In 1995, President Clinton signed Presidential Decision Directive 39, which set the framework for the U.S. policy on counterterrorism. This directive defines responsibilities for various federal agencies, such as the FBI, the Federal Emergency Management Agency, and the Department of Health and Human Services. In the following year, Congress passed a law directing the Department of Defense (DOD) to help enhance the readiness of federal, state, and local agencies to deal with terrorism involving agents of mass destruction.

EXAMPLES OF BIOLOGICAL TERRORIST INCIDENTS

Date and Site	Group	Incident
April 1997 Washington, D.C.	Counter Holocaust Lobbyists of Zion	Anthrax hoax
May 1992 Minnesota	Minnesota Patriot's Council	Planned to assassinate local law enforcement personnel with ricin
April 1990– March 1995 Japan	Aum Shinrikyo ("Supreme Truth")	Attempted various attacks with botulinum and anthrax
Mid-1980s Sri Lanka	Tamil secessionist group	Threatened to infect humans and crops with pathogens
August 1984 Oregon	Rajneeshee religious cult	Infected 751 people with salmonella in Wasco County
October 1984 Paris, France	Red Army Faction	French authorities find flasks of clostridium botulinum in terrorist safehouse
November 1970 Maryland	Weatherman organization	Sought to steal biological agents from Ft. Detrick to poison a city's water supply
1950s Kenya	Mau Mau	Used plant toxins to kill livestock

In response to the law, the DOD and several other agencies established the Domestic Preparedness Program in the Defense Against Weapons of Mass Destruction. This program has begun training "Metropolitan Medical Strike Teams" in 27 cities—including Denver, Chicago, Washington, Los Angeles, and New York—to deal with chemical, biological, and even nuclear terrorism. Local police, firefighters, medics, and other emergency workers are learning to identify such weapons, assist victims, and carry out any decontamination that might be required, according to a DOD press release. The long-term goal is to train teams in 120 population centers.

In April 1996, the U.S. Marine Corps established the Chemical/ Biological Incident Response Force (CBIRF). Since then, CBIRF has conducted demonstrations of what a CB weapons attack by terrorists might mean and how the force would handle a potential incident. Typically, a response would involve several stages: detecting the causative agent, neutralizing the toxin, decontaminating the affected area, and treating the victims. For the members of a rescue team, the first line of defense against CB agents generally involves the use of respirators or gas masks, which protect against inhalation of chemicals or viruses, and special suits that prevent skin contact.

Under a $32.6 million program, the DOD will set up a multiservice Chem-Bio Quick Response Force of up to 500 personnel who will travel around the country training local officials. Furthermore, the DOD and other federal agencies have designed research-and-development programs to enhance the nation's ability to counter the use of CB agents, and they have improved counterintelligence efforts on terrorist organizations.

For his 1998 budget, President Clinton proposed $61.6 million for the Defense Advanced Research Projects Agency (DARPA), to conduct biological weapons defense research. The money will be spent on developing state-of-the-art detectors and new vaccines against biological agents. Moreover, according to published reports, the Pentagon's Quadrennial Defense Review allocated about $1 billion in 1998 toward preparedness against threats from chemical, biological, and nuclear weapons.

On the international level, treaties banning the use of chemical and biological weapons now are in effect. The Biological Weapons Convention (BWC) dates back to 1972, and the 1993 Chemical Weapons Convention (CWC) went into effect in April 1997. These treaties are likely to reduce the proliferation of CB agents and make it more difficult to steal or smuggle such weapons. They also serve to indicate global moral repugnance against the use of these weapons. Of course, the treaties by themselves do not guarantee against the use of these agents by groups that may be bent on harming society for narrow political gain.

What lies ahead regarding the menace of CB terrorism? While the threat is likely to continue into the foreseeable future, we can expect greater awareness and proactive responses from federal, state, and local officials, who are increasing their preparedness to deal with CB agents of terror. But can we be completely insulated from CB terrorism? No. The author of *The Eleventh Plague* concludes that, while preventive actions help limit the impact and damage of chemical and biological terrorism, the "protection of a large population against chemical weapons is difficult; against biological weapons, virtually impossible."

| "Predictions . . . that some terrorist groups will increasingly turn to [chemical or biological weapons] are not new and are generally based on rather scant empirical evidence."

THE THREAT OF CHEMICAL AND BIOLOGICAL TERRORISM IS EXAGGERATED

Marie Isabelle Chevrier

Marie Isabelle Chevrier argues in the following viewpoint that the likelihood of an attack involving chemical or biological (CB) weapons is exaggerated. She maintains that the threat of CB terrorism is low because terrorists have no intention of killing on a large scale. Furthermore, Chevrier contends, even if terrorists wanted to employ CB weapons in an attack, the technical obstacles to producing such weapons would most likely prevent it. Chevrier is an associate professor of political economy at the University of Texas at Dallas. She is also a member of the Federation of American Scientists Working Group on Biological and Toxin Weapons Verification, whose goal is to find methods of enforcing biological weapon bans.

As you read, consider the following questions:

1. According to Chevrier, why did the Aum Shinrikyo attack in Tokyo result in so few fatalities?
2. What information on the production of CB weapons is available on the Internet, according to the author?
3. In the author's opinion, why do analysts prefer to predict that ominous events will happen?

Excerpted from Marie Isabelle Chevrier, "The Aftermath of Aum Shinrikyo: A New Paradigm for Terror?" *Politics and the Life Sciences*, September 1996. Reprinted with permission.

I can remember exactly where I was when I learned that nerve gas had been released in the Tokyo subway, just as I recall my whereabouts for other catastrophic events, such as the Oklahoma City bombing or the Challenger disaster. My initial reaction was disbelief: "It can't be nerve gas," I thought, "*not enough people are dead.*" Only later did I learn that the nerve gas was diluted, of poor quality, and ineffectively dispersed, all of which contributed to the relatively low number of fatalities. Jonathan Tucker, in his article "Chemical/Biological Terrorism: Coping with a New Threat," brings us a vivid account of the subway attack and Aum Shinrikyo, the group which planned and carried out the event. . . .

One of Tucker's principal arguments is that we face an increased likelihood of chemical and biological terrorism from groups like Aum Shinrikyo, which, according to Tucker, is a "new type of terrorist organization, combining elements of a doomsday cult and a large-scale criminal enterprise.". . .

Indeed, one could examine the aftermath of the Tokyo subway attack and reach widely divergent conclusions concerning its effect on other groups considering C/B terrorism. Many analysts conclude that a strong taboo against chemical terrorism, and by extension biological terrorism, was broken. Once the taboo has been broken, the theory goes, more C/B incidents and more deadly incidents are sure to follow. A second inference is that technological difficulties, including those encountered by Aum that limited the number of fatalities, could reasonably be overcome.

AN INTENT TO SHOCK, NOT KILL

On the other hand, one could look at Aum's experience in an entirely different light. Aum Shinrikyo, with over a billion dollars in assets and the ability to recruit scientists and purchase sophisticated equipment, did not plan and carry out an attack that produced massive fatalities. Perhaps Aum did not want to kill in large numbers, but to shock in large numbers. Perhaps the technical hurdles, which Tucker concludes are still substantial, continue to be a binding constraint, especially for biological terrorism. While J.E. Stern states that the risk of failure for a terrorist group is "minimal," the empirical record is marked by many incidents of failure. Furthermore, there may be many more failures that we have never heard of; whereas, there are no hidden successes, at least in terms of chemical weapon (CW) attacks or those with large numbers of casualties.

Similarly, I question whether the willingness of members of

some messianic religious cults to commit mass suicide is necessarily evidence that the members of such groups are willing to turn their destructiveness outward. The connection between the two types of violence—suicidal and homicidal—seems tenuous at best. Moreover, suicide, even on a massive scale, can generally be carried out more quickly, or impulsively, than a complicated plan to kill a large number of people using chemical or biological weapons (CBW). The time and effort involved in planning and executing a CBW attack would usually allow much greater opportunity for reflection and development of reservations than mass suicide.

Tucker reports that in addition to mail-order access, "deadly cookbooks are also available on the Internet." However, the ease with which a terrorist could download a foolproof recipe for C/B weapons from the World Wide Web may be exaggerated. An afternoon surfing the Net yielded the following: the table of contents of The Anarchist's Cookbook and The Terrorists' Handbook, but not the actual texts; and The Jolly Roger Cookbook, which was filled with instructions on how to construct all sorts of explosives, but nothing resembling even World War I vintage chemical weapons. . . . A number of the sites that Tucker mentions, including one with "a recipe for the home production of botulinum toxin," were either gone from the Net or not available using several search engines. The nature of the Internet is that information available yesterday may be gone tomorrow and vice versa. In spite of the widespread repugnance triggered by the availability of this type of information—including the presumably more reliable instructions for explosives—it seems unlikely that any group that could obtain the equipment and personnel skilled in carrying out a C/B attack would rely on the Internet for accurate instructions on production or dispersal of the weapons. A site containing frequently asked questions about The Anarchist's Cookbook noted that it contained numerous factual errors, including the chemical formula for alcohol. . . .

PLANNING FOR A WORST CASE SCENARIO

The prospect of terrorist groups or individuals using chemical or biological weapons—whether or not great numbers of fatalities ensue—is indeed dire. Yet predicting the future, particularly when those predictions involve low probability events, is fraught with uncertainty. Additionally, analysts would certainly rather predict or suggest that ominous events will happen, and be proven wrong, than to be circumspect about the likelihood of disaster and be similarly proven wrong. The consequences of error are much more serious in the latter case than in the former. Consequently, we see a proliferation of "worst case scenario" planning and repeatedly hear the adage, "plan for the worst; hope for the best."

A Huge Undertaking

Anyone who wants to strike a city by spraying anthrax from a plane would need a crop duster with custom-built nozzles that could accommodate germ particles between 1 and 5 microns in size. Particles smaller than that would not have enough mass to float in the air properly. Bigger particles would not be properly absorbed into the lungs.

To generate high casualties, the anthrax would have to be turned into freeze-dried form, which can yield potencies of 100%. But freeze-drying requires complicated, costly equipment that can handle the spores in airtight containers. Only government bioweapon programs, such as Iraq's, are likely to have such equipment.

Paul Richter, *Los Angeles Times*, June 20, 1998.

With the prevalence of this type of thinking, it is not surprising that the release of a liquid containing a nerve gas by the Aum Shinrikyo group in Tokyo has prompted Tucker, as well as other, less scholarly, writers to conclude that we are facing a new threat—that of chemical/biological terrorism. Their predictions—that some terrorist groups will increasingly turn to CBW—are not new and are generally based on rather scant empirical evidence. Indeed, Tucker's list of four criteria that could help predict which terrorist groups might turn to C/B weapons is strikingly similar to a list developed by J.D. Simon seven years ago. [Tucker asserts that terrorist groups may be drawn to CB weapons if they possess the technical know-how, are intent on inflicting mass casualties rather than attracting attention, have no clearly defined base of popular support, and are willing to accept physical risks.]

One argument frequently made is that the public has become inured to terrorists' use of explosives and a terrorist group can no longer fixate the public's attention on its activities with conventional means. Yet the bombing of the Federal Office Building in Oklahoma City demonstrates how effective, and visually riveting, relatively simple explosive devices can be. Perhaps one of the unintended but nevertheless welcome consequences of that bombing is that terrorists need not turn to C/B weapons to command the public's undivided attention or to produce high casualties.

| "The possibility that a rogue state or terrorist organization will use weapons of mass destruction in some unconscionable act has . . . increased."

THE RISK OF NUCLEAR TERRORISM IS HIGH

John Leifer

John Leifer, a consultant and writer based in Kansas City, Kansas, asserts in the following viewpoint that nuclear terrorism is a growing danger. According to the author, the collapse of the former Soviet Union has led to a decline in the security of nuclear storage facilities. As a result, maintains Leifer, Russian nuclear materials are highly vulnerable to theft by terrorists. Furthermore, he contends, information about the construction of nuclear weapons is easily accessible to terrorists. Leifer claims that the deterioration of nuclear security systems, along with the increased accessibility of information on weapons construction, vastly increases the risk of nuclear terrorism.

As you read, consider the following questions:

1. What four key developments does Leifer attribute to the increasing threat of nuclear terrorism?
2. According to the author, how might terrorist groups access information on the construction of nuclear weapons?
3. In the author's opinion, what are two ways a terrorist organization could obtain nuclear materials?

Abridged from John Leifer, "Apocalypse Ahead," The Washington Monthly, November 1997. Reprinted with permission from The Washington Monthly. Copyright by The Washington Monthly Company, 1611 Connecticut Ave. NW, Washington, DC 20009; (202) 462-0128.

The Fall 1997 blockbuster movie "The Peacemaker" pits actors Nicole Kidman and George Clooney against a Bosnian terrorist headed for New York City with a grudge against the West and a backpack full of nukes. The duo's desperate attempts to prevent the bomb-toting villain from pulverizing the Big Apple make for an over-the-top, nail-biting thriller. But although Hollywood has taken its usual artistic license with the film, "The Peacemaker"'s central premise is less implausible than viewers may suspect—and far more possible than government experts and scientists want the public to know.

"I could build a fifteen-kiloton bomb in my kitchen—certainly powerful enough to kill a million people in the middle of Manhattan," says Ted Taylor, one of the chief weapons designers at the Los Alamos National Laboratories during the days when it was still the primary design facility for U.S. nuclear weapons. Taylor is now a professor at Princeton, and like many who've worked in the nuclear field, he's gravely concerned about the prospects of a real-life Peacemaker scenario.

Since the collapse of the Berlin Wall and the progressive dismantling of the Soviet military-industrial complex, Americans bask in the belief that the specter of nuclear destruction is but a vanquished demon, an anachronistic menace that no longer has a place in a post-Cold War world. But although the odds of a strategic nuclear attack may have disappeared along with the former Soviet Union, the possibility that a rogue state or terrorist organization will use weapons of mass destruction in some unconscionable act has, if anything, increased. The growing threat, say physicists, congressmembers, and members of the intelligence community, is the result of the convergence of four key developments: the proliferation of knowledge about how to construct such weapons, the increasing amount of fissile material, the deterioration of the security systems protecting that material, and the changing face of international terrorism.

YOU DON'T HAVE TO BE A ROCKET SCIENTIST

In the late 1970s, a writer named Howard Morland made headlines by publicly unveiling his design for a homemade thermonuclear bomb. Predicated on information gleaned from sources ranging from the *Encyclopedia Americana* to a host of declassified documents, Morland's 270-pound device bore little resemblance to government photos depicting hydrogen bombs as 20-foot long, 20-ton behemoths. Morland's point in developing the schematic was to heighten awareness of the proliferation of potentially dangerous information, and to debunk the belief that weapons of mass destruction were impossibly difficult to either construct or transport. The viability of his amateur schematic—and the validity of his assertions—was made evident when the U.S. government unsuccessfully sued to prevent its publication. (The design eventually ran in the November 1979 issue of The Progressive.)

Morland's schematic was more conceptual than tactical—precise details were missing—leading some skeptics, including a group of scientists assembled by the Nuclear Control Institute (NCI), to assert that a layman still lacks sufficient information to build a bomb. "The detailed design drawings and specifications that are essential before it is possible to plan the fabrication of actual parts are not available," the group pointed out. Furthermore, "the preparation of these drawings requires a large number of man-hours and the direct participation of individuals thoroughly informed [about] . . . the physical, chemical, and metallurgical properties of various materials to be used, as well as the characteristics affecting their fabrication."

But cut through the scientific mumbo-jumbo, and one finds that such knowledge is a lot easier to obtain than these scientists care to admit. For instance, a key piece of information that would-be nuke builders might require relates to the critical mass of fissile material needed to induce fission under select circumstances. Now granted, this is not the type of technical calculation your run-of-the-mill terrorist can work out by conducting experiments in his bathtub. According to Ted Taylor, however, "if someone gets a hold of the Los Alamos critical-mass summaries, he can see how much material is critical in various forms—various ways of shaping the metal, various reflectors wrapped around it." Not planning a trip to New Mexico anytime soon? No problem. Critical-mass summaries can be obtained by writing to the National Technical Information Service in Washington, D.C. "They cost three dollars," offers Taylor.

ACHIEVING A NUCLEAR EXPLOSION

In any event, such detailed information may not even be necessary. Luis Alvarez, a physicist of Manhattan Project fame, claims that if one possesses the right material, even imprecise information is sufficient to achieve a nuclear explosion. "With modern weapons-grade uranium," Alvarez points out in an NCI study, ". . . terrorists, if they had such material, would have a good chance of setting off a high-yield explosion simply by dropping one half of the material onto the other half. Most people seem unaware that if separated U-235 is at hand, it's a trivial job to set off a nuclear explosion. . . . Even a high school kid could make a bomb in short order."

Of course know-how is of little use to a bombmaker if he can't get his hands on the right ingredients. But the actual quantity of fissile material he'll need is pretty small. "The minimum amount of material needed to make a bomb is less than one kilogram of plutonium-239 or three kilograms of uranium-235," notes Taylor. And although a crude bomb constructed by terrorists would most likely require a larger critical mass of fissionable materials, the necessary quantity would still be far from prohibitive. The finished device, says Taylor, would be small enough "to fit in the trunk of a Volkswagen Beetle."

NUKES ON THE LOOSE

What's more, rounding up a bit of fissile material isn't as tough as it used to be, particularly in the destabilized states of the former USSR. In testimony before the Senate in March 1997, Sen. Patrick Leahy (D-Vt.) described a report by the General Accounting Office (GAO) that details the depths to which security at Soviet nuclear waste storage facilities has sunk: "A GAO investigator was able to enter one facility without identifying himself, and there was only one guard present, who was unarmed. There are other descriptions of incredibly lax security that even the most inept thief could easily penetrate undetected. It is almost an open invitation. The implications of this are staggering. A grapefruit-sized ball of uranium, which would weigh about 30 pounds, could obliterate the lower half of the city of New York. A lot more uranium than that is already unaccounted for. We do not know whether it is in the hands of terrorists, or where it is. All we know is that it is missing."

The nuclear weapons situation in Russia is no more comforting, with approximately 27,000 nuclear warheads and 1,300 tons of fissile material lying around, providing a tempting smorgasbord for wannabe terrorists. And in the wake of the USSR's collapse, the vigilance with which this stockpile was once guarded has deteriorated precipitously. Russian Gen. Alexander Lebed recently announced that during a routine inventory, 84 Special Atomic Demolition Munitions, or tactical nukes, were found to be missing from the Russian arsenal. All told, Russia has about 17,000 tactical nukes. Small enough to fit into an average-sized suitcase (making them a prime target for thieves), each bomb is capable of demolishing Manhattan. And even though the U.S., through the Material Protection, Control, and Accounting Program, is working with authorities in the former Soviet states to remove or at least secure the nuclear material lying around in research facilities and nuclear power plants, much of this nuclear material will remain vulnerable to theft or sabotage for years to come. The gravity of the situation is evident to the Russians, if not to our own government: Last October, the director of one of Russia's major nuclear weapons research centers killed himself, explaining in his suicide note that he was no longer capable of guaranteeing the security of the nuclear materials under his supervision.

STOLEN NUCLEAR MATERIALS

According to William Potter, Director of the Center for Nonproliferation Studies at the Monterey Institute of International Studies, in the former Soviet Union alone there have been seven documented cases of significant quantities of bomb-grade nuclear materials being stolen (as opposed to simply disappearing) since the USSR's collapse. And, according to a study conducted by the Harvard-based Center for Science and International Affairs, nuclear material is already being traded on the black market. The study revealed that in August 1994, German police arrested two passengers on a flight from Moscow to Munich who were carry-

Toles. ©1994 The New Republic. Reprinted by permission of Universal Press Syndicate. All rights reserved.

ing a suitcase containing nearly a pound of 87 percent-pure plutonium-239. Likewise, in December of that same year, three kilograms of highly enriched uranium (87.5 percent pure) were seized in Prague, along with Soviet nuclear documents.

These were not isolated events. According to the Center for Strategic and International Studies (CSIS) report, "during a three-and-one-half month period in mid-1992, a chemical engineer named Leonid Smirnov stole approximately 3.7 pounds of HEU (90 percent enriched) from the Luch Scientific Production Association at Podolsk, Russia. Smirnov, who had been employed at the Luch plant since 1968, removed HEU from the plant on 20–25 separate occasions, each time using a 50–70 gram jar." And the list goes on.

In a destabilized region undergoing profound economic and social transformations, such acts of theft are inevitable. As Senator Sam Nunn stated in testimony delivered in September 1996, "It is simply unrealistic to assume that the tons of nuclear materials that are improperly secured, along with thousands of out-of-work Soviet weapons scientists and their equipment will never end up in the wrong hands. Add to this new proliferation problem the evidence of possible organized crime involvement in weapons smuggling and you have the ingredients of a full-blown disaster looming on the horizon."

But terrorist groups are not the only ones itching to get their hands on nuclear weapons. Rogue nations like Syria, Iran, and Iraq—many of which are known sponsors of terrorism—are determined to join the nuclear club, even if it requires a little extralegal shopping. For instance, in their new nonfiction book *One Point Safe* (on which "The Peacemaker" was loosely based), authors Andrew and Leslie Cockburn describe how Iraqi leader Saddam Hussein's son Qusay leads a special covert unit charged with purchasing nuclear missile parts on the Russian black market.

Other Sources for Nuclear Material

Nor is the Soviet Union the only source of nukes for these nations. The raw ingredients they need to construct a viable weapon are often as close as the nearest nuclear power plant—located either within their own borders or in neighboring countries. Certain types of nuclear reactors, known as "breeders," produce a surplus of plutonium in a form that can be readily converted into weapons-grade material. The International Atomic Energy Agency (IAEA) is supposed to ensure that the nuclear material these plants use and produce is directed toward peaceful purposes only. But as Paul Leventhal, founder of the

Nuclear Control Institute and former staff director of the Senate Nuclear Regulation Subcommittee, points out: "The IAEA acknowledges in its technical safeguards documents that, due to measurement uncertainties, its nuclear-accounting system cannot with confidence detect the diversion of bomb quantities of nuclear materials."

The technology is out there, the raw materials are plentiful—so just how worried should we be? Would a terrorist group that got its hands on a nuclear weapon actually dare to use it against us? Recent events speak for themselves: The World Trade Center bombing, the Aum Shinrikyo attack on the Tokyo subway, and the destruction of the Murrah Federal Building in Oklahoma City all point to a major shift in the sophistication and tactics of the world's fanatics. Bruce Hoffman, an analyst for the Rand organization, suggests that these events are a portent of what is to come: "The March 1995 deadly nerve gas on the Tokyo underground marks an historical watershed in terrorist tactics and weaponry. Previously, most terrorists had an aversion to the esoteric and exotic weapons of mass destruction popularized in fictional thrillers or depicted in action-hero movies and television shows. Indeed, the pattern of terrorism over three decades suggests that many groups are impelled by an inner dynamic, an organizational imperative, towards escalation."

Not only has the terrorists' modus operandi changed, but so, too, have their capabilities. Heretofore, it was erroneously presumed that terrorist organizations lacked the requisite infrastructure or resources to engage in nuclear terrorism. Yet the Aum, who were actively exploring the use of nuclear weapons, built an organization with 50,000 adherents, $1 billion in assets, and a staff of elite scientists—all without raising alarm. A congressional permanent subcommittee on investigations was shocked to find "that the Aum and their doomsday weapons were simply not on anybody's radar screen."

THE BATTLE PLAN

The proliferation of nuclear material and weapons, the destabilization of the Soviet regime, the vulnerability of American targets, and the growth of fanatic groups and rogue states have all combined to move us ever closer to nuclear disaster. So what's a conscientious superpower to do? The first, most important step: place greater emphasis on the control of fissile material.

To its credit, the Clinton administration has taken a stab at addressing the problem. It has convinced the former Soviet republics of Ukraine, Belarus, and Kazakhstan to give up their nuclear weapons (though not all their nuclear materials) in exchange for economic assistance. And it has helped physically remove more than 1,300 pounds of highly enriched uranium from Kazakhstan. There remains, however, much to be done. Our only hope of preventing an apocalyptic terrorist event is through a multi-step program that first moves to secure the existing stockpiles of fissile materials, then works to develop organizations with the skills and infrastructure to prevent terrorist attacks. Among the actions the U.S. should take:

1) Develop a systematic method of providing physical protection for existing stockpiles of fissile materials that exist throughout the world. This method may include rendering this material "inactive" through innovative encasement procedures, or in the case of highly enriched uranium, through dilution with non-fissile uranium isotopes. The United States must also insist that such standards for containment are adopted by the global nuclear community; otherwise, they will be of little value.

2) Develop a set of international protocols for the transfer of fissile materials that includes a method of tracking their whereabouts during transit.

3) Create an international intelligence organization capable of monitoring and responding to threats of nuclear terrorism. . . .

Congress, and the American people, need to fully awaken to the challenge and the danger that face us. Nuclear terrorism is a global threat that will require a coordinated international response. The United States released the nuclear genie; it has an obligation to take the lead in stuffing it back in the bottle.

| "Not a single instance has occurred in which a non-governmental group or individual has come anywhere close to obtaining a nuclear weapon— whether by theft or by the construction of a 'homemade' device."

THE RISK OF NUCLEAR TERRORISM IS OVERSTATED

Karl Heinz Kamp

In the following viewpoint, Karl Heinz Kamp contests the notion that nuclear terrorism is becoming a serious threat. Kamp argues that there is no reason to believe that terrorists, who have never utilized nuclear weapons in previous attacks, will turn to them in the future. He contends that it is not in terrorists' interests to commit acts of mass murder, nor is it in their power to construct nuclear devices. Kamp is the head of foreign and security policy at the Konrad-Adenauer-Stiftung, a German political organization that works to maintain democracy.

As you read, consider the following questions:

1. How does Kamp define nuclear terrorism?
2. According to the author, what false assumptions encourage the belief that nuclear terrorism is a serious threat?
3. What obstacles do terrorists face in attempting to construct a nuclear weapon, in Kamp's opinion?

Reprinted from Karl Heinz Kamp, "An Overrated Nightmare," The Bulletin of the Atomic Scientists, July/August 1996, by permission of The Bulletin of the Atomic Scientists. Copyright 1996 by the Educational Foundation for Nuclear Science, 6042 S. Kimbark Ave., Chicago, IL 60637, USA. A one-year subscription is US$28.

A re we entering an "age of superterrorism," as a 1994 report commissioned by the U.S. Defense Department predicts? And how real is the prospect of nuclear terrorism?

Since the collapse of the Soviet Union, some Western security experts have been warning that it is only a matter of time before "loose nukes" in Russia fall into the hands of nuclear terrorists. Stories about the exploits of a "nuclear mafia" are a staple of the tabloid press, and mainstream publications speculate that politically motivated terrorists or international crime syndicates could resort to nuclear blackmail to threaten Western industrial nations. During his campaign for the Republican presidential nomination, Sen. Richard Lugar predicted acts of nuclear terrorism against U.S. targets within this century.

In 1993, Germany recorded 234 incidents of suspected smuggling of an assortment of nuclear-related materials. Then, with the seizure of 300 grams of plutonium at the Munich airport in August 1994, it appeared that—for the first time—there was solid evidence that weapon-grade material was coming on the market.

In early 1995, two startling and tragic acts of terrorism created more intense concerns. What would have happened, we asked, if the lunatics in Oklahoma City had had a nuclear warhead? And what would have happened if the Aun sect in Japan had had not only brilliant chemists, but also physicists and technicians—in other words, nuclear experts?

THE OLD IS NEW AGAIN

The idea of nuclear terrorism is not new. It was an element in the risk analyses of Western security policies long before any illegal trading in nuclear materials was detected. In 1983 Ronald Reagan cited the threat of nuclear terrorism—among other dangers—to justify the Strategic Defense Initiative. President Bill Clinton has also invoked nuclear terrorism as a reason for his administration's interest in "counterproliferation."

Nonetheless, little meaningful analysis of the risk of nuclear terrorism has been undertaken. This discrepancy may result in part from the fact that nuclear terrorism falls into a "high risk–low probability" category—it is a risk whose consequences are serious but whose probability must be rated very low.

Now, however, to the degree that the dissolution of the Soviet empire has altered that risk—particularly to the extent that it may have an impact on European security—the issue of nuclear terrorism deserves another look.

Whether the term "nuclear terrorism" is used in a journalistic or a political context, it is rarely defined. Risk analysts usually talk about "rogue nations," "nuclear violence," "terrorist groups," and "terrorist states" all in the same breath. But this conflates very different actors and actions. The first step is to establish a clear-cut notion of what we mean by nuclear terrorism:

The "nuclear" in nuclear terrorism usually describes an act employing a nuclear device or targeting a nuclear facility. It is also used more broadly to include actions like releasing radioactive substances or contaminating drinking water.

Although any of these acts could take on an apocalyptic character, they differ fundamentally in nature, intensity, and possible methods of prevention. On these pages, I focus only on the possibility that evokes the greatest fear and has been the subject of the greatest speculation—a terrorist threat to use a nuclear device.

In assessing that threat, analysts often confound the issue by throwing in a discussion of rogue states or "terrorist governments." This is inappropriate. Preventing additional states from gaining access to nuclear weapons is and has been for decades one of the express purposes of the Nuclear Non-Proliferation Treaty (NPT) and the international nonproliferation regime. The international community discourages the spread of nuclear weapons to new states with a program of export controls and nuclear accounting.

If a "rogue nation" procured nuclear weapons, the international community would respond in the same way that it would respond to any other perceived threat of war or attack. (Consider the international community's response to Iraq's nuclear ambitions.)

An effort by individuals or groups of individuals to create fear or terror with a credible threat to use—or by actually using—nuclear devices is more properly considered nuclear terrorism. And in contrast to its approach to proliferation, the international community has no organized program for responding to a violent nuclear crime by a group not under state control.

Restricting the definition of nuclear terrorism to non-state actors may significantly reduce the scope of the topic, but by clearing the air of confusing generalizations, it will allow for more specific conclusions.

So Far So Good

As plausible as it may seem that terrorists would consider the threat of nuclear destruction as the ultimate means of enforcing their demands, there has never been a genuine nuclear threat. Not a single instance has occurred in which a non-governmental group or individual has come anywhere close to obtaining a nuclear weapon—whether by theft or by the construction of a "homemade" device. Every past attempt at nuclear blackmail—most of which have occurred in the United States—has been a deception or a bluff, as have been the few nuclear threats that have occurred in Europe.

How can we reconcile the frequent expressions of fear of nuclear terrorism with a history in which not a single incident has occurred?

One explanation may lie in the fact that fears regarding nuclear terrorism are based on several assumptions that are accepted at face value. On closer examination, the truth of these assumptions seems less obvious.

For instance, it is tacitly assumed that terrorists regard nuclear devices as desirable instruments in their political struggles—in other words, we assume that they want nuclear weapons. And we further assume that, if terrorist groups want nuclear weapons, they are in a position to get them, either by producing the weapons themselves or by obtaining them illegally from others. In other words, we assume that they both *want* and *can possess* nuclear weapons.

Another assumption taken at face value is that radical or extreme states (certain states in the Near and Middle East in particular) would willingly help terrorist groups to attain nuclear weapons.

Add to this the assumption that the destabilization of the former Soviet Union, which has led to increased smuggling activities including the sale or smuggling of assorted nuclear materials, means that weapon-grade fissile materials are available on the black market.

If all these assumptions were true, we would have to ask why terrorists do not possess nuclear explosive devices today.

WHAT TERRORISTS WANT

The historical record shows that most nuclear threats have been made by mentally disturbed people, with an occasional bluff by a criminal. Up to now, terrorists have apparently not seriously attempted to seize nuclear weapons. This seems somewhat surprising because the nuclear threat—idle or not—still makes its appearance in international politics. Recent threats include those by Russian nationalist Vladimir Zhirinovsky and the leader of the Bosnian Serbs, Radovan Karadzic, both of whom have threatened to use nuclear weapons against "the West."

Terrorists are willing to use violence—and are indifferent to the possibility that their acts can make victims of innocent by-standers. In fact, the more victims of a terrorist's action, the more likely it is that it will capture the world's headlines.

Yet a review of the world's terrorist incidents shows that those with a high death toll—like the detonation of a bomb on a Pan Am jumbo jet over Lockerbie, Scotland, in 1988, and the explosions at the World Trade Center in New York and the federal office building in Oklahoma City—are relatively rare. The majority of the world's terrorist incidents result in few or no casualties.

And grisly as the worst incidents have been, no terrorist acts have been committed on a scale of truly indiscriminate mass murder—which, given the vulnerability of modern industrial societies, terrorists could achieve or try to achieve without nuclear weapons. (The poisoning of a big-city water supply with chemical agents is often cited as a potential terrorist act of such magnitude.)

Why hasn't such an incident occurred? One explanation is that the terrorists' main objective is to attract as much attention as possible, not to create as many victims as possible. As Brian Jenkins noted in the Autumn 1985 issue of *Orbis*, "Terrorists want a lot of people *watching*, not a lot of people *dead*."

In addition, any mass murder that claimed the lives of those in whose interests the terrorists claim to act, or with whom solidarity is allegedly sought, would inevitably lead to an estrangement between the terrorists and their sympathizers. (This factor is most likely to restrain organizations like the German Red Army Faction or Italy's Red Brigades, who fight against alleged grievances at home and rely on active or passive support from sympathizers in the domestic population.)

A MATTER OF PROPORTION

Another problem concerns the ultimate objective of a nuclear threat. In the case of nuclear blackmail, the goal would have to be truly staggering, because less important goals, like the release of comrades from prison, can be achieved without anything as extreme as a nuclear threat.

Although the objective of a nuclear threat might be truly monumental, it must still be realistic enough that a government could actually fulfill the terrorists' request. Long-term aims could be pursued, but a demand may not be maintained over a long period of time—sooner or later the terrorists would be located and eliminated. Concessions made by blackmailed governments can always be revoked.

This is not to say that terrorists will not want nuclear weapons in the future. There has been a recent increase in transnational terrorism in which fanatic Islamic activists have been willing to carry out suicide operations. And the societies that support these terrorists often regard it as a bonus if as many "enemy" civilians as possible are killed. In addition, the attacks in Oklahoma City and Tokyo may mark a turning point in the sense that a new type of terrorism, one that employs more technical means, is emerging.

NOT SO EASY

The second assumption—that terrorists will make homemade bombs—depends on the popular notion that, since the design of nuclear weapons and their technical principles are well known, it is a distinct possibility that criminal groups or individuals will build their own.

This assumption has been encouraged by statements made by various U.S. government agencies. For example, in 1977 a study by the Office of Technological Assessment concluded that a very small group without secret information could produce a basic nuclear explosive device. And a year later, the U.S. Senate Committee on Governmental Affairs was told that under certain circumstances, an individual—in possession of the proper materials—could design a nuclear weapon. In addition, there have been a stream of reports since the 1970s about gifted physics students or journalists who have compiled usable nuclear weapon designs from freely accessible information.

THE "LOOSE NUKES" MYTH

Since the Soviet collapse, the American public has been bombarded with the "loose nukes" myth . . . that bomb-grade materials—highly enriched uranium or plutonium—are leaking out of Russia. In fact, there is no evidence of any significant leakage of fissile material. . . .

Most importantly, there is absolutely no evidence that nuclear weapons themselves are leaking from Russia. Rumors in 1992 that Kazakhstan sold two tactical nuclear weapons to Iran have been discredited by U.S., Russian, Iranian, and Kazak officials.

William C. Martel, *USA Today Magazine*, March 1997.

Reports of nuclear smuggling appear to lend added weight to the idea that terrorists can build their own bombs, because they suggest that fissile material may now be obtained on a nuclear black market. After all, if gram quantities of uranium 235 and plutonium 239 have appeared on the market, it seems likely that larger quantities are also available. And in view of remarks made by readily quoted "experts"—that one kilogram of plutonium is enough to piece together a nuclear weapon—it would seem virtually inevitable that some terrorist group will build a bomb.

But the idea that terrorists can readily build a bomb is naïve. After all, a number of countries with vast resources and a wide range of scientific and technical personnel have struggled unsuccessfully to produce nuclear weapons. Iraq's nuclear program, which was exposed after the Persian Gulf War, is an example of a costly, time-consuming, and ultimately unsuccessful quest for a nuclear device.

Iraq began recruiting nuclear experts in the early 1970s, and used its worldwide trade links and an elaborate secret procurement network in an effort to obtain the necessary technology. Failing at more advanced methods, Iraq eventually turned to an extremely energy-intensive technology—"calutrons"—that the United States had used to produce uranium in the 1940s. Still, after spending 20 years and more than a billion dollars, Iraq had yet to produce a functioning weapon by the time it was defeated in 1991. It is difficult to imagine that a small terrorist group or an individual—who would certainly have far fewer resources—would find bomb building easier.

THE RIGHT STUFF

Obtaining weapon-grade fissile material is only the first step in building a bomb—nuclear weapons require a host of other "exotic" raw materials. And the amount of fissile material needed depends on the level of accessible technology. As a rule, the more basic the design of a nuclear weapon, the more fissile material required.

It is true that some weapons need no more than a single kilogram of plutonium, but these are weapons produced only in the huge nuclear laboratories of the superpowers, the United States and Russia. And they require technologies like supercompression, which have not yet been mastered by other Western nuclear powers, let alone by any non-governmental nuclear aspirants.

Apart from producing or obtaining fissile material, the production of a weapon requires highly qualified personnel with special know-how in the fields of physics, chemistry, metallurgy, and electronics. Special technical apparatus and complex components are needed that cannot be purchased off the shelf. This applies in particular to plutonium components, which must be machined to exacting technical demands. It is almost absurd to fear terrorist bombs made from smuggled plutonium.

More basic nuclear weapon designs—so-called "gun-type" devices—use only uranium 235. And gun-type designs require masses of fissile material—quantities that go far beyond any amount that has reportedly been offered on a black market.

THE IMPORTANCE OF MISTRUST

In view of the technical complexity of producing nuclear weapons, which is rarely achieved by states, let alone by non-governmental groups, the next question is whether terrorists could obtain the support they would need from countries that back their other activities. After all, "state-sponsored terrorism" is a reality not limited to the Near and Middle East, where "rogue nations" (Iran, Iraq, Libya) have carried out terrorist acts they themselves organize, or have provided support for foreign terrorist groups. After the fall of the Berlin Wall, suspicions were confirmed that the East German government had supported terrorist groups like the Red Army Faction.

Ordinarily, close cooperation between terrorists and sponsoring states can be profitable to both sides. Terrorists receive not only material and logistical support, they also find a safe haven for training and/or recreation. Rogue states can supply terrorist groups with the means to eliminate opponents or to destabilize inimical regimes. And, since it is difficult to prove the relationship between a nation and a terrorist organization, states that sponsor terrorism rarely have reason to fear retaliation.

But it seems doubtful that this model of state-sponsored terrorism would be followed wholesale in the case of nuclear terrorism. There are some fairly serious impediments to a state's willingness to sponsor nuclear terror.

Given the record so far, it seems unlikely that any sponsoring state would willingly "pass along" nuclear know-how or nuclear weapons. Every country that possesses nuclear weapons attaches overriding importance to the control of its nuclear arsenal. When it comes to nuclear weapons, the relations between nuclear and non-nuclear allies—even in NATO—involve security arrangements that imply deep distrust. The security of nuclear weapons and their protection against abuse or unauthorized use have the highest priority and are guaranteed by extensive technical and organizational measures by every current member of the "nuclear club."

Would a state that achieved nuclear capability choose to put nuclear weapons into the hands of terrorists, knowing that a dangerous group could turn against its own patron? The idea that any state—"rogue nation" or not—would hand over the control of nuclear weapons to an organization of criminals or religious zealots is nearly inconceivable.

We cannot rule out the possibility that a nuclear state would sponsor nuclear terrorism, but it seems relatively unlikely.

STOLEN WEAPONS

Many analysts now argue that the technical and organizational difficulties of producing weapons no longer matter, because terrorists will bypass those problems by stealing complete weapons—and then the risk of nuclear terrorism will be a reality.

Even a rare lapse in security in a country with roughly 30,000 warheads could be catastrophic, and there has been a progressive disintegration in organizational structures in the former Soviet Union. As controls have been loosened in Russia's nuclear sector, concern has intensified about the possibility that terrorists could steal a complete nuclear weapon or obtain one from corrupt military personnel or go-betweens.

Well, maybe. But it must be noted that the military organizations responsible for nuclear weapon security in the former Soviet Union have proven more reliable than feared a few years ago. There has been no illegal passing on of complete nuclear weapons or key components. And none of the reports about the marketing of ex-Soviet nuclear materials has involved critical items taken from weapon stocks.

There seem to be two decisive reasons for the stability of the ex-Soviet nuclear weapons sector, particularly in Russia. First, even if Russian leaders did not take Western fears about nuclear weapon security seriously, they would still be concerned about the risks that uncontrolled nuclear proliferation could pose to their own country. As far as possible, resources have been channeled into the nuclear armed forces sector to guarantee its workability. Soldiers in this sector are better paid and facilities have been better maintained than in other areas.

Second, the military's nuclear elites have met very high standards in the past. It is hard to imagine that nuclear units trained during the Soviet era would neglect their tasks under hostile conditions and abuse the goods placed under their command. It would be extremely difficult for terrorists to steal complete nuclear weapons from depots or to obtain them with the help of security personnel. Of course, there is no guarantee that the current stability in the military nuclear sector will continue in the indefinite future.

However, even if a terrorist organization managed—perhaps by working with illegal arms dealers—to obtain a complete nuclear weapon from ex-Soviet stocks, it could not necessarily detonate that weapon. Apart from the fact that most nuclear weapons would be highly unsuitable for terrorist use—due to their size and the difficulty of transporting them—nuclear weapons have a series of built-in technical and security safeguards, including self-destruct mechanisms that can be overridden only by a small and specially trained circle of technicians. Soviet strategic nuclear weapons are secured by systems similar to the sophisticated "Permissive Action Links" (PALs) used to secure U.S. weapons. PALs prevent unauthorized or accidental use by employing multi-digit code systems to lock nuclear weapons against detonation. The United States provided the Soviet Union with the relevant technical know-how for these devices in the early 1960s. To make a credible threat, terrorists would not only have to seize a nuclear weapon, they would have to number in their ranks someone with specific knowledge about a particular explosive device. That possibility cannot be ruled out, but it is highly unlikely in view of the combination of requirements.

Apart from the risk of contamination if nuclear materials are smuggled or stolen, it is more likely that the greater risk arising from the instability of the successor republics of the Soviet Union is that a state on the nuclear threshold—a state that possesses the will, resources, and corresponding facilities—will obtain useful nuclear materials. A threshold state would be best able to incorporate vagabond nuclear material or individual technical components—or even to integrate complete nuclear warheads into an ongoing weapons development program.

For terrorist organizations, the problems of production and/or detonation of nuclear explosive devices represents a threshold that, while it may have been lowered by the uncontrolled movement of some nuclear capabilities from the former Soviet Union, is still extremely difficult to cross.

AND YET . . .

If there is no cause for the hand-wringing that has emerged in connection with reported cases of nuclear smuggling in Europe, there are many imponderables, particularly in respect to potential developments in the former Soviet Union.

Although the probability is low, the cost of nuclear terrorism is grave enough to deserve continuing attention; hectic political activity following specific incidents of nuclear trafficking is not very useful. Many preventive measures aimed at containing the proliferation of nuclear weapons are effective only if pursued over the long term. Continuing Western financial assistance and transfers of protective know-how to states new to nuclear disarmament is important. And "reactive" steps should be planned—measures that can be taken if there are clear indications of nuclear terrorism or similar nuclear emergencies.

The United States has special units trained to handle nuclear emergencies and acts of nuclear terrorism. "Nuclear Emergency Search Teams" (NESTs) have operated under the aegis of the Energy Department for many years. These teams have special technical equipment used to measure radiation and identify radiation sources, and the teams can move to any location in the United States at extremely short notice. Apart from their training in searching for sources of radiation, these teams have also been trained to make exact identifications of materials, defuse nuclear weapons, limit damage if an explosion occurs, and decontaminate irradiated areas.

But Germany, the site of many reports of nuclear smuggling from the former Soviet Union, has no similar organization. Germany has never had nuclear weapons, and those weapons stationed on German soil are controlled by the United States and Britain, and are guarded by U.S. soldiers. Until the collapse of the Soviet Union, American organizations were responsible for dealing with nuclear emergencies.

Given the nature of nuclear terrorism, combating it should be undertaken by Western security alliances, not by individual countries. NATO has already taken on nuclear terrorism with its announcement of the long-term development of military options against the use of weapons of mass destruction by non-state actors. But this is only a first step in developing a comprehensive Western approach to counter nuclear-related threats from terrorist organizations.

It is important that funds be made available to secure or destroy fissile materials and for anti-smuggling and anti-terrorist efforts. Prevention of nuclear terrorism and other nuclear risks cannot be ignored until there is a crisis. They must be perceived as long-term risks that demand continuing attention.

PERIODICAL BIBLIOGRAPHY

The following articles have been selected to supplement the diverse views presented in this chapter. Addresses are provided for periodicals not indexed in the *Readers' Guide to Periodical Literature*, the *Alternative Press Index*, the *Social Sciences Index*, or the *Index to Legal Periodicals and Books*.

Paul Beaver	"The Looming Chemical Weapons Threat," *Wall Street Journal*, December 31, 1997.
Richard K. Betts	"The New Threat of Mass Destruction," *Foreign Affairs*, January/February 1998.
John Deutch	"Combating the Threat of Nuclear Diversion," *USA Today*, January 1997.
Joseph D. Douglass Jr.	"Chemical and Biological Warfare Unmasked," *Wall Street Journal*, November 2, 1995.
David Hughes	"When Terrorists Go Nuclear," *Popular Mechanics*, January 1996.
Susan Katz Keating	"We Lost New York Today," *American Legion Magazine*, June 1997. Available from The American Legion, PO Box 1055, Indianapolis, IN 46206.
William C. Martel	"Puncturing the 'Loose Nukes' Myth," *USA Today*, March 1997.
Bruce W. Nelan	"Nuclear Disarray," *Time*, May 19, 1997.
Bruce W. Nelan	"The Price of Fanaticism," *Time*, April 3, 1995.
Douglas Pasternak	"American Colleges Are 'Weapons U.' for Iraq," *U.S. News & World Report*, March 9, 1998.
Charley Reese	"Stop Worrying About Terrorism," *Conservative Chronicle*, January 28, 1998. Available from Box 37077, Boone, IA 50037-0077.
A.M. Rosenthal	"Only a Matter of Time," *New York Times*, November 22, 1996.
Russell Shaw	"Bio-Bombs Are Biggest Threat," *Insight*, October 7–14, 1996. Available from 3600 New York Ave. NE, Washington, DC 20002.
Robert Tayler	"The Bio-Terrorist Threat," *World Press Review*, September 1996.
Jose Vegar	"Terrorism's New Breed," *Bulletin of the Atomic Scientists*, March/April 1998.

CHAPTER 2

WHAT POLICIES SHOULD THE UNITED STATES ADOPT TOWARD NUCLEAR WEAPONS?

CHAPTER PREFACE

Nuclear weapons, with their capacity to annihilate entire cities and ravage surrounding populations with disease, are regarded by many as inherently dangerous, even evil. According to former nuclear weapons designer Theodore B. Taylor, the possession of nuclear weapons consists of a "preparation for mass murder that cannot be justified under any conditions." Taylor is among those who believe that nuclear weapons are a serious threat to global security and should therefore be completely eliminated. In a joint statement on nuclear weapons, over 50 international generals and admirals assert that "the continuing existence of nuclear weapons in the armories of nuclear powers . . . constitute[s] a peril to global peace and security and to the safety and survival of the people we are dedicated to protect."

However, not everyone sees the abolition of nuclear weapons as a realistic or desirable goal. According to some defense experts, the very destructiveness of nuclear weapons is their greatest benefit: The threat of nuclear retaliation deters both the use of nuclear weapons and warfare in general. As one weapons expert states, "Because nuclear weapons reduce all-out warfare to madness, and because any general war risks escalation to that, advanced states realize that they must not fall into armed conflict with one another." Furthermore, disarmament opponents argue, since nuclear weapons technology and information is readily accessible to both nations and terrorists, abolishing all nuclear weapons would be impossible.

The ideological conflict over nuclear abolition fuels much of the debate on U.S. nuclear policy. The question of how the United States should deal with its own nuclear arsenal is discussed in the following chapter.

| "The elimination of our nuclear weapons would not be good for the United States or for the world."

THE UNITED STATES MUST RETAIN A SUBSTANTIAL NUCLEAR ARSENAL

Robert G. Spulak Jr.

In the following viewpoint, Robert G. Spulak Jr. argues that the United States should retain all of its nuclear weapons. He contends that a strong nuclear arsenal deters attacks on the U.S. and bolsters U.S. influence around the world. Spulak is a senior analyst at the Strategic Studies Center of Sandia National Laboratories, a national security laboratory that designs non-nuclear components of nuclear weapons, conducts energy research, and studies national security threats. He has authored numerous reports on weapon systems, technologies, and policies related to national security.

As you read, consider the following questions:

1. In the author's opinion, why are nuclear weapons stigmatized?
2. According to Spulak, why are nuclear weapons uniquely effective for deterring attacks?
3. Why is credibility important in maintaining a nuclear deterrent, in the author's view?

Excerpted from Robert G. Spulak Jr., "The Case in Favor of U.S. Nuclear Weapons," *Parameters*, Spring 1997. Endnotes in the original have been omitted in this reprint. Reprinted with permission.

As America searches for meaningful diplomatic and military policies to protect and promote its interests in the post-Cold War world, there are essentially two poles of opinion with regard to nuclear weapons. First, there is the post-Cold War status quo, represented by the Clinton Administration's Nuclear Posture Review, conducted in 1993–94, which recommended few and minor changes from Bush Administration policies. And, second, there is an earnest attempt to delegitimize nuclear weapons by minimizing their role, their numbers, and their importance, spreading a kind of nuclear stigma. . . .

Among proponents of nuclear stigma, there is an overarching presumption that it would be a good thing if the world could be made free of nuclear weapons, including our own. In contrast to the cautious recommendations of the Nuclear Posture Review, policies of stigmatizing nuclear weapons are seen to be positive measures that can approach the ideal of a nuclear-free world, despite our inability to put the genie back in the bottle. These pejorative perceptions of nuclear weapons, should they prevail, would represent a shift in the attitudes of policymakers. Whereas most were once convinced of the necessity of nuclear weapons to form the bedrock of strategic deterrence and to counter the conventional might of the Warsaw Pact, the nuclear stigma philosophy is grounded in an optimistic academic debate about nuclear weapons in a less threatening world.

The purpose of this viewpoint is to point out that the nuclear stigma philosophy lacks careful consideration of both the risks *and benefits* associated with nuclear weapons. In fact, the true risks of nuclear weapons seem to be obscured at the same time that the benefits are assumed to have all but disappeared. Any policy made without full recognition of these risks and benefits is likely to have some serious unintended consequences.

ASSESSING NUCLEAR DANGER

Nuclear stigma is an attempt to deal with the dangers associated with nuclear weapons. And indeed, there are many such dangers: danger of all-out nuclear war, danger of unauthorized use, danger of loss of U.S. power relative to proliferating nations, danger of nuclear use by an irresponsible nuclear state, danger of accidental detonation. Although these and other dangers vary widely in consequences, likelihood, and many other characteristics, discussions of "reducing nuclear danger" tend to gather some or all of them under one heading and attempt to characterize them collectively. The policy recommendations to counter them usually include: sanctioning nuclear deterrence only against nuclear attack on the United States; no reliance on nuclear weapons for international political purposes; elimination of extended deterrence; an end to fissile material production; a comprehensive test ban; no strategic defense (tactical missile defenses may be okay); much smaller weapon stockpiles and deployments; and no first use. Authors typically appeal to the power of international institutions to guarantee security and to reduce and eventually eliminate the need for nuclear weapons.

Some of these recommendations may be good, some may be bad, and some may be irrelevant to the actual dangers of nuclear weapons. . . . Many of the recommendations to "reduce nuclear danger" actually could work at cross purposes. One of the most worrisome proposals—for a minimal U.S. strategic stockpile—could actually interfere with nonproliferation by withdrawing extended deterrence from nuclear-capable allies who might then be motivated to develop their own nuclear deterrents. And although it's probably a minor consideration, a comprehensive test ban might even interfere with the ability of existing or new nuclear states to improve the safety of their weapons, increasing the likelihood of accidental detonation.

A MINIMAL STOCKPILE IS NOT ENOUGH

Insistence on minimizing the numbers of nuclear weapons provides a good illustration of the conceptual and analytical problems related to stigmatizing nuclear weapons. Reducing the numbers of weapons might reduce the chances of nuclear war and improve the overall safety and security of our nuclear arsenal—but then again, it might not. Deterrence of war is one of the benefits of nuclear weapons discussed below; for now it is enough to assert that actions that undermine the credibility of our deterrent may make nuclear war more, rather than less, likely in the long run. Many of the other risks associated with nuclear weapons depend upon such aspects as the details of individual weapon designs, the security of the facilities where they are stored, the operational requirements of their delivery systems, and the design and integrity of the nuclear command and control system. If careful attention is not paid to all of these factors, reducing the numbers will not necessarily reduce the real dangers associated with nuclear weapons. In fact, an evident lack of interest in these kinds of nuclear issues at the highest levels in the U.S. government could produce consequences far more important—and far more dangerous—than the number of weapons or the amount of nuclear material the United States possesses.

Further, a minimal stockpile, minimal deterrence, or a doctrine of defensive last resort intended to deter only the use of nuclear weapons is not enough. In any war between major powers there is too great a possibility of unprecedented, virtually terminal, devastation to civilization and mankind. The existence of nuclear weapons creates the risk of catastrophe, but it also creates the only way to ameliorate that risk by minimizing the possibility of war between the major powers. Nuclear weapons have this dual nature: they are the only possible solution to the problem they pose. . . .

THE BENEFITS OF NUCLEAR WEAPONS

There are some who may be uncomfortable with ascribing benefits to weapons of mass destruction. However, these are not simply benefits devoid of risks. There is, in fact, a competition of "alternate risks": the risks of various kinds that arise from having nuclear weapons and the equally serious spectrum of risks that would result from not having nuclear weapons. Possession of nuclear weapons creates benefits that can help to offset the risks of not having them.

Some argue that because of the collapse of the Soviet Union we cannot use history as any guide to the benefits of nuclear weapons. However, with the end of the Cold War neither the nature of the risks nor the nature of the benefits has changed in any fundamental manner. The nature of the benefits of nuclear weapons depends on the characteristics of the weapons themselves and on the need of the United States to have the capability to use force and the threat of force to protect our interests in a world where other nations will always have nuclear weapons. Some very important risks, such as the immediate risk of large-scale nuclear war, have indisputably declined in magnitude, at least for a time. The balance between risks and benefits has shifted, allowing the changes that have already been implemented in U.S. nuclear posture, such as the withdrawal of most tactical weapons from Europe, the elimination of aircraft standing alert, and the elimination of tactical weapons on U.S. ships. But it does not follow that with the end of the Cold War the benefits of nuclear weapons have therefore disappeared and that the United States has no need to have the capability to use or threaten force to protect our interests. Before proceeding with truly revolutionary changes in nuclear policy, any formulation should carefully balance both the risks and the benefits of nuclear weapons.

Possession of nuclear weapons by the United States has historically been very useful (even, some would say, vital to the preservation of freedom in the world). Nuclear weapons are arguably the major reason why the second 45 years of the 20th century did not witness the massive devastation of the world wars of the first 45 years. According to Malcolm Rifkind, "The immense power of nuclear weapons removed, long ago, any rational basis for a potential adversary believing that a major war could be fought in Europe and won. . . . The value of nuclear weapons in such circumstances lies not in classical concepts of war-fighting or war-winning, nor just in deterring the use of nuclear weapons in an adversary, but in actually preventing war."

CONTINUING RATIONALE FOR NUCLEAR DETERRENCE

A principal rationale for maintaining a credible and effective nuclear weapon posture is based on the need to provide a hedge—an insurance policy—against a reversal in relations with Russia and China. Over time, both of these nuclear states have demonstrated a tendency for radical shifts in their political orientation, as well as an enduring commitment to possess nuclear weapons both for the status they afford and as an essential part of their security strategy.

Neither Russia nor China would today seriously consider eliminating their nuclear arsenals, although they would both likely see real value in a unilaterally disarmed United States. . . .

While Americans wring their hands over the pros and cons of dramatic reductions in U.S. nuclear forces, and even debate whether or not to go to zero nuclear weapons, the Russians and Chinese are modernizing their own nuclear forces. In the case of China, this entails building new missiles and warheads, recently tested. In the case of Russia, whose conventional forces are in desperate condition, nuclear modernization includes not only new missiles but elaborate and extraordinarily hardened command and control facilities. Russian doctrine today places more emphasis on nuclear weapons than did Soviet doctrine, as evidenced by Moscow's reversal of its long-standing no-first-use policy. The obvious point is that, given the inability to control or predict where these two states will be in five or ten years, it is essential to hedge against a reversal in relations. And the best hedge is to maintain a nuclear deterrent.

Robert G. Joseph and John F. Reichart, *Orbis*, Winter 1998.

Even those who emphasize other aspects of the historical superpower standoff must include nuclear deterrence high on the list of factors. Nuclear deterrence does not ensure peace, but, short of nuclear war, places a limit on the level of violence. In fact, among great powers the nuclear era has been a most peaceful time. Nuclear weapons appear to have ended the terrible era of ever-more-devastating total war and substituted a relatively less-destructive era of limited war. It was largely the United States' nuclear deterrent that prevented the Soviet Union from realizing the expansionist ambitions it proclaimed to be its obligation as the vanguard of world communism.

An Effective Method of Deterrence

Nuclear weapons are uniquely effective for deterrence because they are enormously destructive and can be delivered in swift retaliation. No other military capability can duplicate the effectiveness of nuclear deterrence. There have been assertions that advanced, precision-guided, conventional weapons can perform the strategic missions of nuclear weapons, but careful analysis shows this idea to be without merit. Our nuclear arsenal is *strategically sufficient*: it can destroy the sources of an enemy's economic, political, and military power. Precision conventional weapons cannot. In addition, for effective deterrence, the image of a single aircraft bunker in the cross hairs of a guided bomb is no match for the evocative image of a mushroom cloud. If we pretend that conventional weapons could be strategically sufficient, we allow the credibility of our nuclear deterrent to be damaged.

The need for nuclear deterrence will not disappear. There are still powerful nations in the world which are potential adversaries, both immediate and future. The interests of these other nations will, at times, be in conflict with the interests of the United States. It is inevitable that another great power or a coalition of powers will arise to oppose the hegemony of the United States. Although the Cold War is over, Russia still has the capability to destroy the United States; the strong showing of the nationalists and communists in the Russian elections, the obvious failure of reforms, the desire of Russia to be recognized as a great power, and replacement of the reformers in the Russian government with officials from the communist era have refocused our concerns on this point. In a few years Japan, a Western European state, or China could pose a strategic threat to our broad security interests; China is rapidly modernizing its arsenal and could soon be a strategic nuclear threat. Since we will be cautious about attacking any nuclear power with conventional forces, it will be difficult to deter even smaller nuclear powers such as North Korea, Iran, or Iraq if our nuclear threat to them is not credible.

Credibility is important for deterrence because the conditions under which the United States would actually use nuclear weapons, and therefore the conditions under which nuclear deterrence even exists, depend on limitations we place on ourselves. Credibility has been one of the most important aspects of nuclear policy from the beginning. For example, the lack of credibility of the U.S. policy of massive retaliation led to the more limited U.S. doctrines that were then developed. The development of warfighting capabilities as a contribution to deterrence was based on the need to demonstrate that there was a likelihood that nuclear weapons would actually be used. . . . Minimizing and stigmatizing our nuclear weapons can create a self-imposed taboo with respect to even nuclear adversaries, thereby delegitimizing deterrence and inviting threats to our interests.

This self-injury to our nuclear deterrence is not the delegitimization of all nuclear weapons that the proponents of nuclear stigma hope for. It is neither reciprocal with our potential enemies nor permanent, even for ourselves.

Credible nuclear deterrence is robust, not delicate. Policies and actions that establish credibility couple with our nuclear arsenal to create the possibility that in a war with the United States an enemy may face a risk of annihilation. A potential enemy need not even be very rational to be deterred from actions that ensure his own destruction. (This is not to argue for belligerence; we can keep the threshold for nuclear use high without undermining credibility.) This creates extreme caution in the behavior of other states if they wish to threaten vital U.S. security interests, and it substantially reduces the likelihood of miscalculation. . . .

BOLSTERING U.S. INFLUENCE

By virtue of their enormous destructive potential, the possession of nuclear weapons creates a quantum increase in power and influence for the United States. Possession creates a threshold of antagonism which no nation can cross. Global awareness of the existence of this threshold allows the United States to exercise influence without the threshold ever being approached. Just as important, the opposite is also true: stigmatizing and minimizing our nuclear weapons can undermine, to some extent, our international status and therefore our ability to influence world events and to protect and promote our interests.

This is important because it matters which states exercise power in the world. (Suppose Nazi Germany had won World War II or the Soviet Union had won the Cold War.) The collapse of the Soviet Union leaves the United States as the only major power whose national identity is defined by a set of universal political and economic values. Sustained U.S. power is central to the future of freedom, democracy, open economies, and international order in the world. . . .

My point is certainly not to argue against encouraging nonproliferation and democracy. These favorable policies generally serve the interests of the United States and most of the other nations of the world. But democracy and nonproliferation are not primary means to achieve security. They can contribute to, but cannot be allowed to dominate unquestioned, the true end of U.S. nuclear policy, which is to provide for the security of the United States including addressing the various risks related to nuclear weapons. The world in which all the great or nuclear powers are liberal democracies does not exist and perhaps never will. It would be unwise to risk the existence of our nation on the fragile notion that democracies will dictate international affairs and, consequently, exist in peaceful union. It is especially unwise to allow wishful thinking to guide policy. Nuclear weapons cannot be disinvented; we will have to live with them, perhaps forever. U.S. nuclear weapons policy should not be constructed upon a mirage of disarmament sentiment.

THE PROBLEMS WITH NUCLEAR STIGMA

There are many different kinds of danger associated with nuclear weapons, including the danger that policies which minimize and stigmatize nuclear weapons may exacerbate old threats and introduce new threats to U.S. security. All choices involve risk. Stigmatizing all aspects of nuclear weapons may blind us to the extent that we overlook policies that could actually reduce the danger of war or violence to the United States and the rest of the world. This concept therefore interferes with our ability to formulate good policies to deal with national security and with the myriad issues related to nuclear weapons.

Since we absolutely cannot achieve the goal of abolishing both nuclear weapons *and* the knowledge of how to construct them, policies and actions that appear to move in that direction will always fail the test of plausibility. But since these policies and actions would be undertaken in the name of "reducing nuclear danger," they acquire a respectability that they have not earned through critical examination. This is the reason it is necessary to reject the emotional appeal reflected in Les Aspin's assertion in 1992 that, in the new era, "the burden of proof is shifting toward those who want to maintain" policies supporting U.S. nuclear weapons and away from those who advocate "four prescriptions of the left . . . a comprehensive test ban, an end to production of fissile material . . . removal of forward-based tactical weapons, and renunciation of first use." An assumption that the formulation of U.S. security policy is biased *a priori* toward a given set of policy recommendations is exactly the problem with nuclear stigma.

NUCLEAR WEAPONS SHOULD NOT BE ELIMINATED

The benefits of U.S. nuclear weapons support the argument that the elimination of our nuclear weapons would not be good for the United States or for the world. These benefits include deterrence against attacks on our central security interests, a contribution to the general prevention of war, extended deterrence that protects our allies and discourages proliferation, security against technological surprise, maintenance of our superpower status, and the tangible benefits of nuclear diplomacy.

This is not to say that there are no national security problems associated with U.S. nuclear weapons. A serious discussion that attempts to balance the dangers *and* benefits of nuclear weapons must be undertaken before dramatically altering our security policy. Wishing that nuclear weapons didn't exist will not alter the security needs of the United States or the associated nuclear problems. The United States needs to exercise wise leadership in formulating its policies and in promoting and protecting its worldwide interests. Policies of minimizing and stigmatizing the sources of our strength will only make it more difficult to lead.

| "Just a few hundred warheads might satisfactorily fulfill [the] core deterrent function [of nuclear weapons]."

THE UNITED STATES SHOULD REDUCE ITS STOCKPILE OF NUCLEAR WEAPONS

William F. Burns

William F. Burns contends in the following viewpoint that the diminished threat of nuclear war presents an opportunity for the United States to significantly reduce its nuclear arsenal. According to Burns, the U.S. should restrict the role of nuclear weapons to deterring or responding to a nuclear attack. Burns, a retired United States Army major, was the director of the U.S. Arms Control and Disarmament Agency under President Ronald Reagan. He chaired a study by the Committee on International Security and Arms Control of the National Academy of Sciences, which produced the report *The Future of U.S. Nuclear Weapons Policy*.

As you read, consider the following questions:

1. According to the author, what changes have the United States and Russia made to their nuclear policies since the end of the Cold War?
2. In Burns's view, why should the role of nuclear weapons be restricted to that of deterring a nuclear attack?
3. What short-term measures does the author propose for reducing nuclear danger?

Reprinted from William F. Burns, "The Unfinished Work of Arms Control," *Issues in Science and Technology*, Fall 1997, pp. 37–40, by permission of *Issues in Science and Technology*. Copyright 1997 by the University of Texas at Dallas, Richardson, Texas.

In the half century since Hiroshima and Nagasaki, the world has experienced no further use of nuclear weapons in conflict. Indeed, the restraint the major powers exercised in avoiding conventional war among themselves could very well have been due to the cautionary influence exerted by the existence of nuclear weapons. But the nuclear weapons era has entailed considerable costs and dangers—above all, the risk that the unimaginable destruction of nuclear war would be unleashed by accident or error or by escalation from a conventional conflict or a crisis. Also, the risk has always been present that the major powers' prominent reliance on nuclear deterrence and the possible use of nuclear weapons in war fighting would promote nuclear proliferation among more and more countries.

With the Cold War over, the danger of premeditated nuclear war with Russia has practically disappeared, and the conventional military threats once thought to require deterrence with nuclear weapons are likewise much diminished. The United States and Russia have taken advantage of these fundamental changes with a series of major agreements and unilateral initiatives. Under the terms of the first Strategic Arms Reduction Treaty (START I), signed in 1991 and currently being implemented by both countries, the number of strategic nuclear warheads deployed by the two sides will be cut from 13,000 and 11,000, respectively, to about 8,000 each. START II, signed in 1993, would further limit the number of deployed strategic warheads to 3,000 to 3,500 on each side; the United States ratified the treaty in early 1996, but Russia has not yet done so. At the Helsinki summit in March 1997, Presidents Bill Clinton and Boris Yeltsin agreed to seek a START III treaty with a level of 2,000 to 2,500 deployed strategic nuclear warheads. Unilateral initiatives since the early 1990s have also significantly reduced the numbers of deployed nonstrategic warheads, especially on the U.S. side. Nuclear testing has ended and the United States and Russia have agreed not to target their missiles against each other on a day-to-day basis. Perhaps most important, a debate has begun on the proper role and function of nuclear weapons in the long run.

NUCLEAR POLICIES HAVE NOT CHANGED

Despite this remarkable progress in reducing the number of nuclear weapons, neither the basic character of U.S. and Russian nuclear forces nor the plans and policies for their use have fundamentally changed from what they were during the Cold War. This leaves us with nuclear postures, and associated costs and risks, out of proportion to the diminished demands on these forces in the post–Cold War world. For example, both the United States and Russia continue to maintain a significant portion of their nuclear forces in a state of alert that would permit them to launch thousands of nuclear warheads in a matter of minutes. These continuous-alert practices exacerbate the risk of erroneous or unauthorized use. As long as one side maintains its forces in a state of high alert, it is politically unrealistic to expect the other side to lower its guard. And Russia has announced that, to offset the weakness of its conventional forces, it is adopting for its nuclear weapons a "first-use-if-necessary" doctrine similar to that of the United States and NATO, thus apparently giving nuclear weapons a more central role in its national security.

Moreover, the size of these arsenals, even after START I and (we hope) START II are implemented, will remain larger than necessary for deterrence. Also, the risk that other countries might obtain nuclear weapons remains serious and requires continuing high-priority attention.

THE ROLE OF NUCLEAR WEAPONS

To respond fully to the opportunities to reduce nuclear dangers opened by the end of the Cold War, the United States should adopt a fundamental principle: The role of nuclear weapons should be restricted to deterring or responding to a nuclear attack against the United States and its allies—that is, the United States would not threaten to respond with nuclear weapons to attacks by conventional, chemical, or biological weapons. Limiting nuclear deterrence to its "core function" would permit significant measures to further reduce the risks posed by nuclear weapons, including changes in nuclear operations and improvements in the safety and survivability of nuclear weapons. Adequately sized and properly equipped conventional forces would be essential in providing an effective response to nonnuclear threats. Consonant with this approach, of course, the United States must meet its own security requirements and its commitments to friends and allies. And it must take great care to reassure its allies that those commitments will be kept.

Since the Persian Gulf War, there has been considerable discussion about whether nuclear weapons should be used to deter chemical and biological weapons. It is a serious misnomer to lump the three types of weapons together under the label "weapons of mass destruction." In reality, these are very different types of weapons in terms of lethality, of certainty of destruction, and of their relative effectiveness against military targets. Chemical and especially biological weapons are serious and growing problems for international security. But nuclear weapons are not the answer to the most likely uses of chemical and biological weapons against the United States or its allies.

ADOPTING A DOCTRINE OF NO FIRST USE

Restricting nuclear weapons to the core deterrence function would permit a number of significant changes. First, the United States should make no first use of nuclear weapons its explicit doctrine—and encourage Russia to do the same—rather than continuing to adhere to "first use if necessary" for nuclear weapons. This would allow for much deeper reductions in the U.S. nuclear arsenal. Provided that the remaining nuclear forces are survivable and their command-and-control systems are robust, just a few hundred warheads might satisfactorily fulfill this core deterrent function. Reaching such low levels will obviously have to be accomplished in stages, and very significant improvements in our verification capabilities will be required to ensure that small numbers of nuclear weapons are not hidden away for deleterious purposes. Also, other countries, both declared and undeclared nuclear powers, must be included in a regime of nuclear arms reductions before the United States and Russia could prudently reduce the number of their warheads below 1,000.

Among the short-term measures to be taken, two seem particularly important to restore momentum toward fulfilling the unfinished agenda of reducing the nuclear danger.

JUMP-START START

Serious discussions should begin immediately to outline the details of the proposed START III agreement, rather than waiting for START II to take effect. The current policy of demanding Russian ratification of START II before discussions begin gives the Russian Duma too much leverage over the arms control process and could cause unnecessary delay when (and if) ratification is achieved.

In addition, START III should be negotiated under the counting rules created in START I and II, which count deployed delivery systems and then assess a count of deployed strategic warheads indirectly, in order to enable us to reach early agreement. The difficulty of agreeing on the details of a change to counting total warheads—and actually doing the counting—is more of a burden than the next round of reductions should have to bear. Future agreements beyond START III, however, should encompass all nuclear warheads: strategic and nonstrategic, active and reserve.

Prune the Nuclear Hedge

The 1994 Nuclear Posture Review, carried out by the Department of Defense, is the basis of current U.S. policy. A key factor in the review's conclusions was the perceived need to retain U.S. flexibility in case reform in Russia failed. As a result, the United States opted to maintain a "hedge" of additional reserve warheads to provide the ability to reconstitute its nuclear forces if it became necessary. But additional firepower would not improve the practical deterrent effect of U.S. nuclear forces in the event of renewed antagonism with Russia. Moreover, the need to increase its strategic readiness in ways open to intelligence-gathering systems—for example, by dispersing bombers or by moving a larger fraction of its ballistic missile submarine force to patrol areas—would provide a genuine hedge against surprise. The United States would only need to increase its nuclear force levels if massive growth in the Russian force imperiled the survivability of the U.S. arsenal; for the foreseeable future, Russia has no realistic capability for such reconstitution.

Beetle Bailey. Reprinted with permission of King Features Syndicate, Inc.

The primary risk posed by the hedge strategy is that it could become a self-fulfilling prophecy: The United States may consider keeping a substantial stock of reserve warheads a matter of prudence, but to Russia it could look very much like an institutionalized capability to break out of the START agreements. To the extent that the United States is concerned about a return to hostile relations with Russia, it should focus on decreasing the probability of such perceptions.

Abandoning the hedge would also save several billion dollars a year and ease the burden on the Department of Energy in maintaining the reliability and safety of an oversized nuclear stockpile. In the absence of a compelling security requirement, it makes good budgetary and military sense to reduce the number of warheads.

Two other important short-term measures require serious technical study and analysis to make their implementation possible:

PROVIDE GREATER OPERATIONAL SAFETY

In parallel with but not directly tied to the START III discussions, the United States should begin seeking measures to provide higher levels of operational safety for nuclear weapons. Technical discussions with the Russians should begin as soon as possible so that any unilateral moves might be readily reciprocated. At present, "dealerting"—measures to extend the time it would take to prepare nuclear weapons for launching—is receiving considerable attention. Serious detailed studies are needed from the military-technical community to provide the basis for implementing this idea. And any agreed reduction in alert status would have to be accompanied by reliable means of assuring compliance, an essential element of which would be a warhead accountability system.

Although it is relatively easy to describe the idea of "dealerting," achieving it without destabilizing consequences will not be trivial. To the extent that we are concerned about the safety and security of Russian strategic nuclear forces, however, such measures are the most direct remedy. More broadly, ending continuous-alert practices would be a significant step toward reducing the dangers of a hair-trigger posture.

COUNT ALL WARHEADS

At the Helsinki summit in March 1997, Presidents Clinton and Yeltsin agreed to begin exploring how to move toward a regime that uses warheads—all warheads, not just those deployed—rather than delivery vehicles as the unit of account. This is an essential step for deep reductions in nuclear weapons; countries will not agree to cut their arsenals to minimum levels if they cannot be assured that significant stocks of nuclear warheads are not hidden away. It is also a formidable verification challenge, requiring advances in technology considerably beyond what is available today.

But no verification system could provide complete assurance that no clandestine stocks remained. Therefore, as nuclear reductions proceed to lower levels, the issue of how much uncertainty is acceptable becomes increasingly important. This, in turn, places a greater burden on the international security system to provide confidence that there will be few incentives to cheat and that violations, when detected, will be dealt with swiftly. It emphasizes the necessity for our own security to maintain conventional forces capable of executing whatever tasks they are called on to perform. It also highlights the importance for the United States of maintaining stability through equality with Russia during any prolonged period of reductions.

The unfinished agenda for arms reductions thus includes significant political and technical challenges. But we have found remarkable agreement, both within and outside the government and in the international community as a whole, that this is the agenda that must be pursued. The consensus about the role and future of nuclear weapons has changed dramatically since the end of the Cold War. Many once almost unthinkable policy options have now become issues of "when" and "how," not "whether." Some of the agenda items are controversial and may not be implemented soon. But we are beyond the stage of philosophical debate and into the realm of wrestling to form workable policy choices and strategies to carry them out.

| "A world free of the threat of nuclear weapons is necessarily a world devoid of nuclear weapons."

THE UNITED STATES SHOULD ELIMINATE ITS NUCLEAR ARSENAL

Part I: Lee Butler, Part II: Joseph Rotblat

In Part I of the following two-part viewpoint, Lee Butler, a re-tired general in the United States Air Force, argues in favor of eliminating nuclear weapons. He maintains that the current U.S. policy of retaining a nuclear arsenal for deterrence is unethical, dangerous, and expensive. In Part II, Joseph Rotblat asserts that the nuclear powers must uphold their legal commitment to complete nuclear disarmament. He claims that the abolition of nuclear weapons would significantly reduce the risk of war. Rot-blat, winner of the 1995 Nobel Peace Prize, is the president of the Pugwash Conferences, an organization that brings together international scholars who are seeking cooperative solutions to global conflict. Part II of the following viewpoint is excerpted from Rotblat's Nobel Prize acceptance speech given in Oslo on December 10, 1995.

As you read, consider the following questions:

1. What six concerns does Butler have about the existence of nuclear weapons?
2. According to Rotblat, what steps should be taken toward the elimination of nuclear weapons?

Part I: Excerpted from Lee Butler, "National Press Club Remarks," December 4, 1996. Text available at http://www.stimson.org/generals/but1204.htm. Used with permission of the Stimson Center. Part II: Excerpted from Joseph Rotblat, "Remember Your Humanity," *The Bulletin of the Atomic Scientists*, March/April 1996. Copyright ©1995 by The Nobel Foundation, Stockholm. Reprinted by permission of the copyright holder.

I

I am compelled to speak, by concerns I cannot still, with respect to the abiding influence of nuclear weapons long after the Cold War has ended. . . . I feel the weight of a special obligation in these matters, a responsibility born of unique experience and responsibilities. Over the 27 years of my military career, I was embroiled in every aspect of American nuclear policy making and force structuring, from the highest councils of government to nuclear command centers; from the arms control arena to cramped bomber cockpits and the confines of ballistic missile silos and submarines. I have spent years studying nuclear weapons effects; inspected dozens of operational units; certified hundreds of crews for their nuclear mission; and approved thousands of targets for nuclear destruction. I have investigated a distressing array of accidents and incidents involving strategic weapons and forces. I have read a library of books and intelligence reports on the Soviet Union and what were believed to be its capabilities and intentions . . . and seen an army of experts confounded. As an advisor to the President on the employment of nuclear weapons, I have anguished over the imponderable complexities, the profound moral dilemmas, and the mind-numbing compression of decision-making under the threat of nuclear attack.

THE BURDEN OF NUCLEAR ARSENALS

I came away from that experience deeply troubled by what I see as the burden of building and maintaining nuclear arsenals: the increasingly tangled web of policy and strategy as the number of weapons and delivery systems multiply; the staggering costs; the relentless pressure of advancing technology; the grotesquely destructive war plans; the daily operational risks; and the constant prospect of a crisis that would hold the fate of entire societies at risk.

Seen from this perspective, it should not be surprising that no one could have been more relieved than was I by the dramatic end of the Cold War and the promise of reprieve from its acute tensions and threats. The democratization of Russia, the reshaping of Central Europe. . . . I never imagined that in my lifetime, much less during my military service, such extraordinary events might transpire. Even more gratifying was the opportunity, as the commander of U.S. strategic nuclear forces, to be intimately involved in recasting our force posture, shrinking our arsenals, drawing down the target list, and scaling back huge impending Cold War driven expenditures.

Most importantly, I could see for the first time the prospect of restoring a world free of the apocalyptic threat of nuclear weapons.

Over time, that shimmering hope gave way to a judgment which has now become a deeply held conviction: that a world free of the threat of nuclear weapons is necessarily a world devoid of nuclear weapons. Permit me, if you will, to elaborate briefly on the concerns which compel this conviction.

First, a growing alarm that despite all of the evidence, we have yet to fully grasp the monstrous effects of these weapons, that the consequences of their use defy reason, transcending time and space, poisoning the earth and deforming its inhabitants. Second, a deepening dismay at the prolongation of Cold War policies and practices in a world where our security interests have been utterly transformed. Third, that foremost among these policies, deterrence reigns unchallenged, with its embedded assumption of hostility and associated preference for forces on high states of alert. Fourth, an acute unease over renewed assertions of the utility of nuclear weapons, especially as regards response to chemical or biological attack. Fifth, grave doubt that the present highly discriminatory regime of nuclear and non-nuclear states can long endure absent a credible commitment by the nuclear powers to eliminate their arsenals. And finally, the horrific prospect of a world seething with enmities, armed to the teeth with nuclear weapons, and hostage to maniacal leaders strongly disposed toward their use.

A Terrible Price

That being said, let me hasten to add that I am keenly aware of the opposing arguments. Many strategists hold to the belief that the Cold War world was well served by nuclear weapons, and that the fractious world emerging in its aftermath dictates that they will be retained . . . either as fearsome weapons of last resort or simply because their elimination is still a Utopian dream. I offer in reply that for me the Utopian dream was ending the Cold War. Standing down nuclear arsenals requires only a fraction of the ingenuity and resources as were devoted to their creation. As to those who believe nuclear weapons desirable or inevitable, I would say these devices exact a terrible price even if never used. Accepting nuclear weapons as the ultimate arbiter of conflict condemns the world to live under a dark cloud of perpetual anxiety. Worse, it codifies mankind's most murderous instincts as an acceptable resort when other options for resolving conflict fail.

Others argue that nuclear weapons are still the essential trappings of superpower status; that they are a vital hedge against a resurgence of virulent, Soviet-era communism; that they will deter attack by weapons of mass destruction; or that they are the most appropriate choice for response to such attack.

To them I reply that proliferation cannot be contained in a world where a handful of self-appointed nations both arrogate to themselves the privilege of owning nuclear weapons, and extol the ultimate security assurances they assert such weapons convey. That overt hedging against born-again, Soviet-style hardliners is as likely to engender as to discourage their resurrection. That elegant theories of deterrence wilt in the crucible of impending nuclear war. And, finally, that the political and human consequences of the employment of a nuclear weapon by the United States in the post-Cold War world, no matter the provocation, would irretrievably diminish our stature. We simply cannot resort to the very type of act we rightly abhor.

A GLOBAL CONSENSUS ON ABOLITION

Is it possible to forge a global consensus on the propositions that nuclear weapons have no defensible role; that the broader consequences of their employment transcend any asserted military utility; and that as true weapons of mass destruction, the case for their elimination is a thousand-fold stronger and more urgent than for deadly chemicals and viruses already widely declared immoral, illegitimate, subject to destruction and prohibited from any future productions?

I am persuaded that such a consensus is not only possible, it is imperative. Notwithstanding the uncertainties of transition in Russia, bitter enmities in the Middle East, or the delicate balance of power in South and East Asia, I believe that a swelling global refrain will eventually bring the broader interests of mankind to bear on the decisions of governments to retain nuclear weapons. The terror-induced anesthesia which suspended rational thought, made nuclear war thinkable and grossly excessive arsenals possible during the Cold War is gradually wearing off. A renewed appreciation for the obscene power of a single nuclear weapon is coming back into focus as we confront the dismal prospect of nuclear terror at the micro level.

Clearly the world has begun to recoil from the nuclear abyss. Bombers are off alert, missiles are being destroyed and warheads dismantled, former Soviet republics have renounced nuclear status. The Non-Proliferation Treaty has been indefinitely extended, the Comprehensive Test Ban Treaty is now a de facto prohibition, and START II may yet survive a deeply suspicious Duma [the

Russian congress]. But, there is a much larger issue which now confronts the nuclear powers and engages the vital interest of every nation: whether the world is better served by a prolonged era of cautious nuclear weapons reductions toward some indeterminate endpoint; or by an unequivocal commitment on the part of the nuclear powers to move with much greater urgency toward the goal of eliminating these arsenals in their entirety.

NUCLEAR WEAPONS MUST BE ELIMINATED

I chose this forum to make my most direct public case for elimination as the goal, to be pursued with all deliberate speed. I firmly believe that practical and realistic steps, such as those set forth by the Stimson Center study, or by the Canberra Commission on the Elimination of Nuclear Weapons, can readily be taken toward that end. But I would underscore that the real issue here is not the path—it is the willingness to undertake the journey. In my view, there are three crucial conditions which must first be satisfied for that journey to begin, conditions which go to the heart of strongly held beliefs and deep seated fears about nuclear weapons and the circumstances in which they might be used. First and foremost, is for the declared nuclear weapon states to accept that the Cold War is in fact over, to break free of the norms, attitudes and habits that perpetuate enormous inventories, forces standing alert and targeting plans encompassing thousands of aimpoints.

Second, for the undeclared states to embrace the harsh lessons of the Cold War: that nuclear weapons are inherently dangerous, hugely expensive, and militarily inefficient; that implacable hostility and alienation will almost certainly over time lead to a nuclear crisis; that the failure of nuclear deterrence would imperil not just the survival of the antagonists, but of every society; and that nuclear war is a raging, insatiable beast whose instincts and appetites we pretend to understand but cannot possibly control.

Third, given its crucial leadership role, it is essential for the United States to undertake as a first order of business a sweeping review of its nuclear policies and strategies. . . .

Options are being lost as urgent questions are unasked, or unanswered: as outmoded routines perpetuate Cold War patterns and thinking; and as a new generation of nuclear actors and aspirants lurch backward toward a chilling world where the principal antagonists could find no better solution to their entangled security fears than Mutual Assured Destruction.

Such a world was and is intolerable. We are not condemned to repeat the lessons of forty years at the nuclear brink. We can do better than condone a world in which nuclear weapons are accepted as commonplace. The price already paid is too dear, the risks run too great. The task is daunting but we cannot shrink from it. The opportunity may not come again.

II

Long before the terrifying potential of the arms race was recognized, there was a widespread instinctive abhorrence of nuclear weapons, and a strong desire to get rid of them. Indeed, the very first resolution of the General Assembly of the United Nations—adopted unanimously—called for the elimination of nuclear weapons. But the world was then polarized by the bitter ideological struggle between East and West. There was no chance to meet this call. The chief task was to stop the arms race before it brought utter disaster. However, after the collapse of communism and the disintegration of the Soviet Union, any rationale for having nuclear weapons disappeared. The quest for their total elimination could be resumed. But the nuclear powers still cling tenaciously to their weapons.

Scott Bateman. Reprinted by special permission of King Features Syndicate.

Let me remind you that nuclear disarmament is not just an ardent desire of the people, as expressed in many resolutions of the United Nations. It is a legal commitment by the five official nuclear states, entered into when they signed the Nuclear Non-Proliferation Treaty (NPT). In 1995, when the indefinite extension of the treaty was agreed, the nuclear powers committed themselves again to complete nuclear disarmament. This is still their declared goal. But the declarations are not matched by their policies, and this divergence seems to be intrinsic.

Since the end of the Cold War the two main nuclear powers have begun to make big reductions in their nuclear arsenals. Each of them is dismantling about 2,000 nuclear warheads a year. If this program continued, all nuclear warheads could be dismantled by 2005. We have the technical means to create a nuclear-weapon-free world by this time. Alas, the present program does not provide for this. When the START II Treaty has been implemented—and remember it has not yet been ratified—we will be left with some 15,000 nuclear warheads, active and in reserve. Fifteen thousand weapons with an average yield of 20 Hiroshima bombs.

The Present Philosophy

Unless there is a change in basic philosophy, we will not see a reduction of nuclear arsenals to zero for a very long time, if ever. The present basic philosophy is nuclear deterrence. This was stated clearly in the U.S. Nuclear Posture Review which concluded that the "post–Cold War environment requires nuclear deterrence," and this is echoed by other nuclear states. Nuclear weapons are kept as a hedge against some unspecified dangers.

This policy is simply an inertial continuation from the Cold War era. The Cold War is over, but Cold War thinking survives. Then, we were told that a world war was prevented by the existence of nuclear weapons. Now, we are told that nuclear weapons prevent all kinds of war. These are arguments that purport to prove a negative. I am reminded of a story told in my boyhood, at the time when radio communication began.

"Two wise men were arguing about the ancient civilization in their respective countries. One said: 'My country has a long history of technological development: We have carried out deep excavations and found a wire, which shows that already in the old days we had the telegraph.' The other man retorted: 'We too made excavations; we dug much deeper than you and found . . . nothing, which proves that already in those days we had wireless communication!'"

Nuclear Weapons Do Not Deter War

There is no direct evidence that nuclear weapons prevented a world war. Conversely, it is known that they nearly caused one. The most terrifying moment in my life was October 1962, during the Cuban missile crisis. I did not know all the facts—we have learned only recently how close we were to war—but I knew enough to make me tremble. The lives of millions of people were about to end abruptly; millions of others were to suffer a lingering death; much of our civilization was to be destroyed. It all hung on the decision of one man, Nikita Khrushchev: would he or would he not yield to the U.S. ultimatum? This is the reality of nuclear weapons: they may trigger a world war; a war which, unlike previous ones, destroys all of civilization.

As for the assertion that nuclear weapons prevent wars, how many more wars are needed to refute this argument? Tens of millions have died in the many wars that have taken place since 1945. In a number of them nuclear states were directly involved. In two they were actually defeated. Having nuclear weapons was of no use to them.

To sum up, there is no evidence that a world without nuclear weapons would be a dangerous world. On the contrary, it would be a safer world.

We are told that the possession of nuclear weapons—in some cases even the testing of these weapons—is essential for national security. But this argument can be made by other countries as well. If the militarily most powerful—and least threatened—states need nuclear weapons for their security, how can one deny such security to countries that are truly insecure? The present nuclear policy is a recipe for proliferation. It is a policy for disaster.

To prevent this disaster—for the sake of humanity—we must get rid of all nuclear weapons.

ESSENTIAL STEPS TOWARD ELIMINATION

Achieving this goal will take time, but it will never happen unless we make a start. Some essential steps towards it can be taken now. Several studies, and a number of public statements by senior military and political personalities, testify that—except for disputes between the present nuclear states—all military conflicts, as well as threats to peace, can be dealt with using conventional weapons. This means that the only function of nuclear weapons, while they exist, is to deter a nuclear attack.

All nuclear weapon states should now recognize that this is so, and declare—in treaty form—that they will never be the first to use nuclear weapons. This would open the way to the gradual, mutual reduction of nuclear arsenals, down to zero. It would also open the way for a nuclear weapons convention. This would be universal—it would prohibit all possession of nuclear weapons.

We will need to work out the necessary verification system to safeguard the convention. A Pugwash study produced suggestions on these matters. The mechanism for negotiating such a convention already exists. Entering into negotiations does not commit the parties. There is no reason why they should not begin now. If not now, when?

So I ask the nuclear powers to abandon the out-of-date thinking of the Cold War period and take a fresh look. Above all, I appeal to them to bear in mind the long-term threat that nuclear weapons pose to humankind and to begin action towards their elimination. Remember your duty to humanity.

| "De-alerting [nuclear] missiles
| would ... make the world safer."

THE UNITED STATES SHOULD REMOVE ITS NUCLEAR ARSENAL FROM ALERT STATUS

Tim Zimmermann

Removing nuclear weapons from alert status would increase the amount of time needed to launch nuclear missiles from minutes to hours. Tim Zimmermann, a contributing editor for U.S. News & World Report, maintains in the following viewpoint that de-alerting nuclear missiles would avert the risk of an accidental or unauthorized firing. Furthermore, he contends, de-alerting would have the added benefit of encouraging the disarmament of U.S. and Russian nuclear arsenals.

As you read, consider the following questions:

1. What instance of a potentially catastrophic mistake is cited by Zimmermann?
2. In the author's opinion, why is the risk of an accidental launch increasing?
3. According to the author, what are the current options for taking nuclear arsenals off hair-trigger alert?

At the height of the Cold War, fears of an accidental nuclear exchange loomed large both in Hollywood and in Washington, D.C. Movies like *Fail Safe* and *Dr. Strangelove* played on the risks posed by communication glitches and rogue commanders. Some policy makers at the White House, the Pentagon, and on Capitol Hill also were concerned about the dangers of maintaining a huge nuclear arsenal on hair-trigger alert. But most accepted the risks as the unavoidable price of deterring the Soviets from launching a massive, surprise attack.

Today, the Cold War is over, and under the framework of the Strategic Arms Reduction Treaty, or START I, the U.S. and Russian strategic nuclear arsenals have been cut by about one-third. Both countries have mothballed thousands of short-range tactical weapons and taken their long-range bombers off standby alert. In 1994, Presidents Bill Clinton and Boris Yeltsin further agreed to stop targeting strategic missiles at each other's country—although this step had little strategic significance because it takes only a few seconds to re-enter targeting coordinates into a missile's guidance system.

Keeping Weapons on Hair-Trigger Alert

Many Americans feel a lot safer. But in fact the danger of nuclear annihilation has scarcely diminished. In their continuing preoccupation with the now unlikely possibility of a first-strike attack, both the United States and Russia have kept thousands of strategic nuclear warheads on hair-trigger alert. Accordingly, both countries together remain ready to fire more than 5,000 warheads within a half-hour's notice.

"It's an anachronism," says Sen. Tom Daschle, a South Dakota Democrat. "My biggest concern is the instability of Russian forces today. . . . There are still a significant number of nuclear weapons that could be [fired at the United States] under mistaken circumstances." He and a growing chorus of experts, such as former Sen. Sam Nunn, want Moscow and Washington to lower the risk of accidental or unauthorized attacks by "de-alerting" their nuclear forces—that is, increasing the amount of time needed to launch missiles from a few pressure-packed minutes to hours or even days.

Near-Fatal Error

Russian President Boris Yeltsin knows all about the potential for a catastrophic mistake. In January 1995, a meteorological missile fired from Norway to study the northern lights activated Russia's early-warning system. Although the Norwegians had notified

Russian officials well before the launch, the message had not been passed along to Russia's high command. Yeltsin and his top generals agonized for several minutes over whether the rocket was part of a surprise U.S. attack. Fortunately, a few minutes short of the deadline for firing a retaliatory salvo, the scientific rocket headed out toward the ocean and away from Russia.

THE NUCLEAR HAIR-TRIGGER

Although international relations have changed drastically since the end of the cold war, both Russia and the U.S. continue to keep the bulk of their nuclear missiles on high-level alert. So within just a few minutes of receiving instructions to fire, a large fraction of the U.S. and Russian land-based rockets (which are armed with about 2,000 and 3,500 warheads, respectively) could begin their 25-minute flights over the North Pole to their wartime targets.

Less than 15 minutes after receiving the order to attack, six U.S. Trident submarines at sea could loft roughly 1,000 warheads, and several Russian ballistic missile submarines could dispatch between 300 and 400. In sum, the two nuclear superpowers remain ready to fire a total of more than 5,000 nuclear weapons at each other within half an hour. . . .

The coupling of two arsenals geared for rapid response carries the inherent danger of producing a mistaken launch and an escalating volley of missiles in return. The possibility of an apocalyptic accident cannot be ruled out even under normal conditions. And if the control of Russian nuclear weapons were to be stressed by an internal or international political crisis, the danger could suddenly become much more acute. During the cold war, such risks were subordinated to the overriding requirement to deter an enemy believed to be willing to launch a nuclear attack. This rationalization is no longer defensible, if ever it was.

Today, when both countries seek normal economic relations and cooperative security arrangements, perpetuating the readiness to launch nuclear weapons on the mere warning of an attack constitutes reckless behavior.

Bruce Blair, Harold Feiveson, and Frank von Hippel, *Scientific American*, November 1997.

The risk of a horrible mistake is only growing with the widening political and economic turmoil in Russia. The loss of former Soviet radar installations that are outside Russia's current borders has left significant gaps in the country's early-warning network, making Russian fingers on the button ever more jittery. Stories abound in Russia of utility companies' shutting off power to nuclear weapons facilities because the military has not paid the bills, and of nuclear control equipment failing because thieves have stolen communications cables for their copper. Morale in the military also has plummeted as a result of chronic food and housing shortages. Indeed, in February 1997, Russia's then defense minister, Igor Rodionov, warned that cuts in defense spending were pushing Russia toward a point "beyond which its missiles and nuclear systems become uncontrollable."

POSSIBILITIES FOR DE-ALERTING NUCLEAR ARSENALS

The Clinton administration is for the first time formally reviewing options for taking U.S. and Russian nuclear arsenals off hair-trigger alert. The possibilities include: taking warheads off missiles and storing the warheads up to hundreds of miles away from the silos; removing missiles' guidance systems (reinstalling them would take expert technicians at least a few hours); and keeping ballistic-missile submarines either in port or at patrol locations well out of range of their targets. Compliance with these measures would be possible to verify through on-site inspections or satellite images.

Deliberately increasing the time needed to launch nuclear weapons would have an added benefit: At a time when the START approach of shrinking the overall arsenal is under increasing attack in the Russian parliament, this would introduce a new approach to arms control. Bruce Blair, a nuclear-command-and-control expert at the Brookings Institution in Washington, D.C., argues that a sensible first step for President Clinton is to immediately de-alert long-range missiles slated for retirement under the stalled START II agreement. If President Yeltsin responded in kind, the two presidents could engage in a virtual disarmament process that, over time, might eventually succeed in dismantling the nuclear balance of terror without going to the controversial extreme of completely eliminating nuclear weapons.

De-alerting missiles would not only make the world safer but could also provide President Clinton with the historic achievement he has long sought. The limited-test-ban treaty is still considered one of the great achievements of the Kennedy presidency. And in a survey conducted last September, reducing the risk of nuclear war ran second only to improving U.S. education as the most important legacy President Clinton could leave his country.

"De-alerting would not only erode the deterrent value of [U.S. nuclear] weapons, but would also invite pre-emptive attack."

REMOVING NUCLEAR WEAPONS FROM ALERT STATUS WOULD JEOPARDIZE U.S. SECURITY

Kathleen Bailey

In the following viewpoint, Kathleen Bailey criticizes proposals to remove U.S. nuclear missiles from alert status. According to Bailey, de-alerting nuclear weapons—that is, lengthening the time needed to launch a missile—would threaten U.S. security. In order to effectively deter a nuclear attack, she claims, the United States must retain an arsenal that is able to be fired immediately. Bailey is a senior fellow at Lawrence Livermore National Laboratory and the former assistant director for proliferation at the Arms Control and Disarmament Agency.

As you read, consider the following questions:

1. According to Bailey, why are U.S. nuclear missiles on alert?
2. In the author's view, why would de-alerting nuclear weapons be destabilizing?
3. What three reasons does Bailey provide for why the proposal to de-alert missiles is being considered?

Reprinted from Kathleen Bailey, "De-alerting Nukes Would Imperil U.S. Security," The Wall Street Journal, January 20, 1998, by permission.

D o you believe the U.S. should maintain a strong nuclear deterrent as long as we face the threat of nuclear, chemical and biological weapons? If so, here's a major cause for worry: The Clinton administration is considering "de-alerting" our nuclear arsenal.

The idea is that the U.S. would make our nuclear-tipped missiles all but unusable through such measures as removing their nuclear warheads or guidance systems. This would erode the U.S. nuclear deterrent and increase the risk of an early nuclear strike against the U.S. Before taking such a step, the dangers should be debated widely and openly, not just behind the closed doors of the executive branch.

The primary reason that U.S. nuclear missiles are on alert—that is, ready to be fired quickly—is that Russia retains as many as 10 times more tactical nuclear weapons than we do, an arsenal capable of destroying the U.S. Although Moscow presently shows no intention of using its nuclear arsenal, this could change quickly given Russia's volatile politics. It is Moscow's nuclear capability—not just its intentions—that must concern us.

There are clear signs that Russia is enhancing these capabilities and that its leadership intends to rely increasingly on nuclear weapons. It is modernizing its nuclear weapons and delivery systems at high cost, despite its financial woes. Moscow's refusal to ratify the START II treaty and its abandonment of its nuclear no-first-use pledge also introduce uncertainty.

THE IMPORTANCE OF A NUCLEAR DETERRENT

Moreover, the U.S. nuclear deterrent protects us not just from Russia but also from other nations' nuclear arsenals, as well as from the chemical and biological weapons proliferating around the world. President Clinton's revision of the nuclear-use doctrine recognizes the growing need to rely on nuclear retaliation to deter attacks with other types of weapons of mass destruction. The speed with which nuclear retaliation can be executed can mean the difference between the U.S. or its allies suffering one chemical or biological weapons attack or many.

Proponents of de-alerting argue that even after its weapons were de-alerted, the U.S. could reconstitute its nuclear missiles and bombs quickly enough to retaliate against an aggressor. This is patently false, even if other powers also agreed to de-alert, because they could cheat on such a deal with virtually no risk of detection. If Russia agreed to disable one set of mobile missile launchers, for instance, it could clandestinely manufacture another set. If it removed one set of warheads, it could secretly produce and upload a second set. Alternatively, Moscow might not declare all of its existing warheads or delivery vehicles. Iraq has already taught us the lesson that mobile missiles are difficult to locate; we can expect that Russian missiles would be equally hard to find. Also, the U.S. currently has no technologies to locate undeclared, hidden stockpiles of nuclear weapons or weapons materials.

CREATING A NEW VULNERABILITY

Some argue that [the U.S. should] remove all weapons from alert status by removing [their] warheads . . . and placing them in a small number of storage sites. But this creates a new vulnerability: these warheads could be destroyed or made unusable through attack by a very small number of enemy warheads, thereby giving an aggressor a unique, dangerous and destabilising advantage. . . . Moreover, if a crisis were to occur, having weapons stored separately from their launchers could generate a race to be first to remate the warheads with their delivery systems. This would be highly destabilising.

Walter Slocombe, *NATO Review*, November/December 1997.

In addition to being unverifiable, de-alerting would be extremely destabilizing. If warheads were removed to storage, for example, they would be consolidated targets, inviting preemptive attack. Also, if the U.S. were to begin to reconstitute its nuclear forces in a period of insecurity—by reinstalling warheads, for example—it would be observable by the enemy and thus could cause crisis escalation.

FLAWED REASONS FOR DE-ALERTING

Why would the Clinton administration consider making U.S. nuclear weapons all but unusable? There are at least three reasons. First, de-alerting is touted as a way to avoid a nuclear exchange begun by an unauthorized or accidental launch from Russia. The idea is that Russia would follow our lead in making nuclear arms more difficult to use.

But the danger of accidental use may be overstated. Air Force Gen. Eugene Habiger, commander-in-chief of the U.S. Strategic Command, visited Russia in November of 1997 and observed that "any one of [Russia's nuclear] command centers, from the national level down to the unit level, can inhibit the launch of an intercontinental ballistic missile." If indeed the threat of unauthorized or accidental launch is real, the better way to address it is through enhancing command and control and by building U.S. missile defenses, not hobbling our deterrent.

Second, de-alerting seems attractive because it would skirt treaty negotiation and ratification processes—both of which are likely to slow the pace of nuclear disarmament. Disarmament advocates have seen the difficulties of getting Russia to ratify START II and are worried about the lengthy, arduous road ahead for START III. De-alerting would denuclearize—for those nations that choose to comply—without lengthy treaty talks or confirmation proceedings by a cautious Senate or Duma.

Third, proponents of de-alerting see it as a step toward nuclear disarmament. Having failed to ban the gun, they want to have the bullets removed.

While disarmament is a noble goal, the U.S. should retain its nuclear deterrent in a highly usable, alert status for as long as necessary to preserve our national security, which is of course an even more important goal. De-alerting would not only erode the deterrent value of our weapons, but would also invite pre-emptive attack.

PERIODICAL BIBLIOGRAPHY

The following articles have been selected to supplement the diverse views presented in this chapter. Addresses are provided for periodicals not indexed in the *Readers' Guide to Periodical Literature*, the *Alternative Press Index*, the *Social Sciences Index*, or the *Index to Legal Periodicals and Books*.

William M. Arkin — "The Bomb Has Many Friends," *Bulletin of the Atomic Scientists*, March/April 1997.

Tom Bethell — "No Nukes America," *American Spectator*, December 1996.

Bruce Blair, Harold Feiveson, and Fran von Hippel — "Taking Nuclear Weapons Off Hair-Trigger Alert," *Scientific American*, November 1997.

Lee Butler — "A Voice of Reason," *Bulletin of the Atomic Scientists*, May/June 1998.

Ashton B. Carter and John M. Deutch — "No Nukes? Not Yet," *Wall Street Journal*, March 4, 1997.

Sam Cohen — "Save the Nukes," *National Review*, February 10, 1997.

Andrew F. Krepinevich Jr. — "Forging a Path to a Post-Nuclear U.S. Military," *Issues in Science and Technology*, Spring 1997.

John M. LaForge — "Nuclear Disarmament," *Z Magazine*, July/August 1998.

Jonathan S. Landay — "Nuclear Disarmament with Low-Tech Approach," *Christian Science Monitor*, February 20, 1998.

Henry Sokolski — "A Blast of Reality," *New York Times*, May 13, 1998.

CHAPTER 3

How Can the United States Defend Itself from an Attack?

CHAPTER PREFACE

In 1983, President Ronald Reagan proposed the Strategic Defense Initiative (SDI), a space-based defense system whose goal was to shoot down enemy ballistic missiles before they could reach United States soil. Such a system, as Reagan conceived it, would include satellites that could detect a massive nuclear launch within seconds, orbiting lasers, laser-equipped submarines, and a ground-based missile system. Congress agreed to fund research for the SDI, but the program was abandoned when the nuclear standoff between the United States and the former Soviet Union came to an end in the early 1990s.

In recent years, however, the idea of building a defense system against ballistic missiles has been rejuvenated. In 1998, Congress allocated funds toward the construction of anti-ballistic missiles—devices that would intercept a foreign missile and destroy it mid-flight. Advocates of the plan maintain that a missile defense system is essential in light of increased weapons proliferation: According to writer Charles M. Calderon, "As many as 25 countries have the technical capability to build a nuclear weapon, and 26 have gained access to long-range missiles." Moreover, contend defense proponents, with hostile nations such as North Korea, Iran, and Iraq rushing to develop new weapons technology, a missile attack on the United States is an increasing possibility.

Those who oppose a missile defense system maintain that only two countries—China and Russia—currently possess ballistic missiles with range long enough to strike the United States, and fear of retaliation would prevent these countries from attempting an attack. Furthermore, critics insist, even if a missile defense were warranted, the system is a scientific impossibility. During the years that the SDI program was funded, opponents note, research failed to produce any devices that could accurately intercept foreign missiles. National security specialist Joseph Cirincione reports that "in tests conducted by the Department of Defense since 1982, only two hits were achieved in 13 attempts against a variety of targets and a range of interceptor systems."

A missile defense system is one proposal aimed at defending against weapons of mass destruction. In the following chapter, authors debate this issue and recommend other ways that the United States can prepare for and defend against an attack involving chemical, biological, or nuclear weapons.

| "The surest way to ensure the safety of U.S. citizens is to deploy a national missile defense capable of protecting the entire nation against . . . missile strikes."

THE U.S. SHOULD ADOPT A BALLISTIC MISSILE DEFENSE SYSTEM

Curt Weldon

Initially developed by President Ronald Reagan in 1983, the proposal to construct and deploy a defense against ballistic missiles is again being debated by legislators. The goal of a national missile defense is to intercept foreign ballistic missiles—which could be armed with nuclear, biological, or chemical warheads—before they could hit the United States. In the following viewpoint, Curt Weldon argues that a ballistic missile defense is the only way to safeguard the United States against threats to its security. Congressional representative Weldon, a Republican from Pennsylvania, is chairman of the Subcommittee on Research and Development, which is part of the House National Security Committee.

As you read, consider the following questions:

1. What examples of instability in Russia does the author cite?
2. According to Weldon, which countries besides Russia pose a threat to U.S. security?
3. In the author's opinion, why are the arguments against deploying a ballistic missile defense implausible?

Excerpted from Curt Weldon, "An Urgent Need for a Missile Defense," USA Today magazine, May 1997. Reprinted by permission of USA Today and the Society for the Advancement of Education, ©1997.

In January, 1996, when Pres. Bill Clinton delivered his State of the Union Address, he spoke of the dawning of a new age in foreign relations, one filled with the promise of peace. He painted the vision of a world in which "not a single Russian missile is pointed at America's children" and North Korea has "frozen its dangerous nuclear weapons."

As much as I wish that peace permanently has been secured, sadly that is not the case. In reality, we live in a world that in many ways is as unstable as at any point during the Cold War. The sole purpose that Pres. Clinton's words served was to lull American citizens into a false sense of security. In fact, the proliferation of weapons of mass destruction is the single greatest threat to our national security, and it only will grow worse. The surest way to ensure the safety of U.S. citizens is to deploy a national missile defense capable of protecting the entire nation against limited or accidental missile strikes.

Many people do not understand the nature of the missile threat to our country. In 1995, during debate of the Defense Authorization Bill, one Congressman asked: "What is the threat? The Power Rangers?" Such comments illustrate how little information some members of Congress—entrusted by constituents to ensure their safety—have about the real threats to the U.S.'s national security and the lives of its citizens.

According to intelligence agencies, it is impossible to verify that the Russian nuclear arsenal no longer is aimed at the U.S. Even if this were possible, Russia could retarget its ballistic missiles toward American cities in less than 60 seconds. The real threat today is not a full-scale nuclear attack, but the accidental or rogue launch of Russian ballistic missiles and the danger of proliferation of ballistic missile technology to rogue nations.

Russia's Instability

As Russia struggles to implement reforms in the post-Soviet era, the command and control of its nuclear weapons have grown frighteningly unstable. Reports indicate that former Soviet soldiers are underfed, underpaid, and highly demoralized. Often, soldiers have resorted to selling ammunition and weapons to buy food or liquor. Another report stated that Russian strategic forces are so short on money that they have to hire out soldiers for menial jobs like digging potatoes, leaving some nuclear missile sites shorthanded and requiring some crews to work double shifts.

It is not surprising that Russian soldiers and officers have grown increasingly embittered at Moscow's treatment of the military. They possess little or no sense of loyalty to the government. One Russian soldier pointed out that "it is pretty reckless on the part of [Russian Pres. Boris] Yeltsin and [former Defense Minister Pavel] Grachev to entrust weapons to youths who are suffering malnutrition, cold, and neglect by their commanders." If Russia's own soldiers are concerned by this problem, the U.S. should be cautious as well. . . .

The most serious example of the instability in Russia came in January, 1995, when Yeltsin admitted to activating his "nuclear briefcase"—a device used for the launching of Russia's nuclear forces in the case of an enemy attack. What was the cause for such an emergency? It turns out that the security scare was the result of a scientific research missile launched by Norway. The rocket launch, which Norway had notified Russia of a month earlier, was detected by Russian early warning systems and prompted a nuclear security alert. That a routine launch would cause such widespread panic is extremely unsettling, as is the statement by a Russian diplomat that "there are many incidents like this that no one knows about."

Of equal concern is the fact that Russia actively is marketing converted, mobile, SS-25 ballistic missiles as space-launch vehicles for satellites. These intercontinental-range missiles are capable of striking any city in the U.S. Should these rockets fall into the wrong hands, it would not require much effort to reverse the process whereby they were transformed from long-range ballistic missiles into space-launch vehicles, making a rogue nation capable of striking American cities. With the Russian government aggressively marketing SS-25s to any nation that can afford them, it is just a matter of time before one falls into the wrong hands. . . .

OTHER THREATS TO THE U.S.

The situation in North Korea is troubling as well. It is developing the Taepo-Dong 2, a missile that, according to intelligence reports, may be capable of striking American cities as early as the year 2000. Successful development of this technology will place the U.S. in the position of being threatened by North Korea and any country to which it makes the missile available. In the past, North Korea has been more than willing to export SCUD-type missiles for hard currency or oil. As the country's Stalinistic economy continues its downward spiral, there is little reason to be hopeful that North Korea would not take advantage of any opportunity to sell this deadly new weapon.

Those who believe that no nation ever would threaten the U.S. with a ballistic missile need look no further than China's attempts to intimidate Taiwan before its presidential election by launching missiles dangerously close to Taiwan's coast. However, another action by China's government went largely unreported in the press—an attempt to use its long-range nuclear weapons to blackmail the U.S. In January, 1996, the Chinese government issued a not-so-veiled threat to Washington, warning it not to interfere in the Taiwan–China conflict since American leaders "care more about Los Angeles than Taiwan."

DANGER FROM THE MIDDLE EAST

Attempts to blackmail the U.S. will increase as more countries obtain ballistic missiles, making it more difficult for America to conduct an effective foreign policy. Libyan leader Muammar Qaddafi, for example, has made it clear that he would not hesitate to use ballistic missiles against the U.S. if his country possessed the capability. Referring to the American bombing of Tripoli and Benghazi in 1986, he remarked to his countrymen: "Did not the Americans almost hit you yesterday when you were asleep in your homes? If they know you have a deterrent force capable of hitting the United States, they would not be able to hit you. Because if we possessed a deterrent, missiles that could reach New York, we would have hit in the same moment. Consequently, we should build this force so they and others will no longer think about an attack."

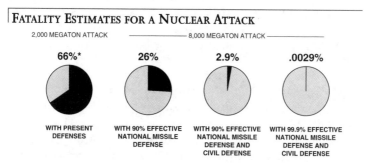

FATALITY ESTIMATES FOR A NUCLEAR ATTACK

2,000 MEGATON ATTACK ——————— 8,000 MEGATON ATTACK ———————

| 66%* | 26% | 2.9% | .0029% |
| WITH PRESENT DEFENSES | WITH 90% EFFECTIVE NATIONAL MISSILE DEFENSE | WITH 90% EFFECTIVE NATIONAL MISSILE DEFENSE AND CIVIL DEFENSE | WITH 99.9% EFFECTIVE NATIONAL MISSILE DEFENSE AND CIVIL DEFENSE |

*Percent of U.S. population that will die as a result of an attack

Conrad V. Chester, *Journal of Civil Defense*, Summer 1993.

Iraqi Pres. Saddam Hussein's comment in 1990 was equally ominous: "Our missiles can not reach Washington. If they could reach Washington, we would strike if the need arose." Fortunately for the U.S., Iraq did not possess an intercontinental ballistic missile capability during the Persian Gulf War. If it had,

Pres. George Bush might have been much less willing to attempt to liberate Kuwait. At the very least, it would have proven much more difficult for the U.S. to form the coalition necessary to oust Iraq from Saddam's so-called "lost province."

It is only a matter of time before rogue nations such as Iraq and Libya obtain the means to threaten American cities with ballistic missiles armed with chemical, biological, or nuclear weapons. Once they do, the results could prove to be disastrous.

THE NEED FOR DEPLOYMENT

For all of these reasons, it is necessary that we deploy a national missile defense capable of protecting all 50 states as quickly as possible. Yet, opponents to such a system have managed to confuse debate on the issue by launching a campaign of misinformation and distortion of the facts regarding the proposed Defend America Act, which calls for the immediate deployment of a national missile defense system.

In leading their charge against the legislation, opponents argue that a national missile defense system would cost tens of billions of dollars. To back up this accusation, they cite Congressional Budget Office (CBO) estimates that a multi-layered missile defense system, with space-based sensors and tracking, could cost up to $60,000,000,000.

In reality, the Defend America Act calls for a national missile defense by 2003 to defend only against a limited missile attack, such as a rogue missile strike or accidental launch. According to another study released by the CBO, we can deploy such a defense, depending on the option chosen, for between $4,000,000,000 and $13,000,000,000.

FALSE ARGUMENTS AGAINST A NATIONAL MISSILE DEFENSE

Another argument that has been raised about the deployment of a national missile defense is that it would require the U.S. to abrogate the Anti-Ballistic Missile Treaty. This is untrue. Under the terms of the ABM Treaty, both the U.S. and Russia are allowed a single anti-ballistic missile site to defend against an attack. Russia has taken advantage of this provision and has deployed a treaty-compliant missile defense system around Moscow. Similarly, there are several treaty-compliant national missile defense options available to the U.S., and Pres. Clinton could choose to exercise any one of them.

An additional argument that opponents unconvincingly have used is that deployment of a national missile defense would be a major impediment to START II ratification in Russia. The true impediment to START II ratification is the issue of NATO expansion, not the deployment of an American missile defense. Yet, the President continues to call for the expansion of NATO out of one side of his mouth while arguing out of the other side that deployment of a national missile defense will undermine START II.

Some may say that proponents of a national missile defense are anti-Russia and are attempting to "stick it in their eye." In my own case, nothing could be further from the truth. As one of the leading proponents of a national missile defense, I often have worked with Russia on issues important to both our countries and in strengthening ties between our two nations. . . .

As someone who has worked extensively with Russia, I obviously am not seeking to deploy a national missile defense to irk its leaders. Furthermore, there is no reason for Russia, with its hundreds of ballistic missiles, to feel threatened by a limited ABM system capable of defending against an accidental or rogue strike.

Even if one ignores all of the threats cited above, it makes no sense to remain undefended until a threat emerges. With the lives of millions of Americans at stake, to wait to deploy a missile defense until we are 100% certain that a threat has emerged is unconscionable. Undoubtedly, it will take a few years to put a defense into place. What if it is deployed too late?

> "National missile defenses [pose] a
> political barrier to deep reductions
> in nuclear arsenals, which remain
> the most effective way to increase
> U.S. and international security."

THE U.S. SHOULD NOT ADOPT A BALLISTIC MISSILE DEFENSE SYSTEM

Lisbeth Gronlund and David Wright

In 1998, Congress adopted a plan to test potential missile defenses—devices that are designed to intercept foreign missiles before they reach the United States. Under this plan, missile defenses will be constructed and tested until the year 2000, when Congress will decide whether to deploy these defenses. In the following viewpoint, Lisbeth Gronlund and David Wright contend that the planned ballistic missile defense system is technologically infeasible and will pose a barrier to reductions in international nuclear arsenals. Gronlund and Wright are senior staff scientists at the Union of Concerned Scientists, a nonprofit alliance of scientists and citizens working for a healthy environment and a safe world.

As you read, consider the following questions:

1. According to the authors, how have the goals of a national missile defense changed from 1983 to 1997?
2. What evidence do Gronlund and Wright provide to prove that a national missile defense will fail?
3. In the authors' opinion, how is Russia likely to view a U.S. missile defense?

Reprinted from Lisbeth Gronlund and David Wright, "The 'Star Wars' Legacy: Big Budgets, Little Progress," Issue Brief, vol. 2, no. 9, March 25, 1998, by permission of the authors and the Coalition to Reduce Nuclear Dangers.

In 1983, President Ronald Reagan announced his "Star Wars" program to build a defense of the United States against attacks by nuclear-armed ballistic missiles. After three Presidents, eight Congresses and some $40 billion, how far has the U.S. national missile defense program come?

Although the goals of the program have been scaled back dramatically, they are still technically infeasible. Despite this, the United States is closer than ever to deploying a national missile defense: it selected a general contractor in March 1998 to develop a system by 2000 that could then be deployed within three years of a decision to do so. This rush to develop a system is termed a "rush to failure" in the February 27, 1998, report of an independent panel appointed by the Defense Department and headed by former Air Force chief of staff General Larry Welch, which is described in stories by The Washington Post on March 22 and 25, 1998.

At the same time, pushing ahead with national missile defenses poses a political barrier to deep reductions in nuclear arsenals, which remain the most effective way to increase U.S. and international security.

U.S. MISSILE DEFENSE GOALS SCALED BACK DRAMATICALLY

1983: The original goal [of a national missile defense], laid out in Reagan's March 23, 1983, speech, was to render nuclear weapons "impotent and obsolete" and to protect the U.S. population from a large-scale attack by thousands of Soviet nuclear warheads.

1987: The original mission is implicitly dropped as unrealistic and the focus shifted from protecting cities to enhancing deterrence by protecting U.S. nuclear weapons from a disarming first strike.

1991: Under President George Bush, a space-based layer of "Brilliant Pebbles" interceptors is added to the plan, but the goal is scaled-back to defending against up to 200 warheads launched at once.

1997: Scaled back once again, the current goal is to defend against only 5 to 20 "simple" warheads, nominally launched by accident or without authorization by Russia or China, or deliberately by a hostile nation that might acquire long-range ballistic missiles in the future. The program might be expanded over time, with the objective of defending against a greater number of warheads.

NATIONAL MISSILE DEFENSE PROGRAM NO CLOSER TO SUCCESS

The technology still isn't ready: Despite the considerable time and money invested, the basic technology for a national missile defense—"hit-to-kill" interceptors that would destroy their targets by ramming into them—is not ready for deployment. The test record for hit-to-kill interceptors has been very poor, even against cooperative test targets. According to a December 1997 General Accounting Office (GAO) report, "Of the 20 intercept attempts since the early 1980s, only 6, or about 30 percent, have been successful." Even more relevant to national missile defenses are the 14 of these intercept tests that were conducted at high altitudes, of which only 2 were hits, for a 14 percent success rate. And the test record is not getting better with time: the most recent successful high-altitude test occurred in January 1991 and the last 9 such intercept tests have been failures.

"IT'LL WORK—THE MISSILES WILL GET CONFUSED BY ALL THAT MONEY BEING SHOT AT THEM"

©1998 by Herblock in *The Washington Post*. Used by permission.

The testing program is inadequate: The planned test program is so meager that the Pentagon won't know how well the system works by 2000, when they may decide to build it. The Pentagon is completely ignoring the "fly before you buy" maxim. As the GAO report notes, only one integrated system test is planned prior to the deployment decision, and even that test will not include all system elements. Similarly, the independent panel headed by General Welch concluded that decisions to accept abbreviated timetables and minimal numbers of flight tests have raised the risk of more failures, delays and cost overruns. Moreover, according to the system engineering contractor, the test program will not adequately test the ability of the system to discriminate warheads from decoys and debris, even though this task would be essential to the successful defense of the United States.

The fundamental problem of countermeasures remains unsolved: A more fundamental problem is that defenses will not face cooperative targets. All defenses that seek to intercept warheads outside of the atmosphere can be defeated by technically straight-forward countermeasures, and this problem remains unsolved despite decades of work. Indeed, this is precisely why the current program objectives call only for defending against "simple" warheads—those without effective countermeasures. However, any country that could build or acquire a long-range missile could also build or acquire effective countermeasures that would require less sophisticated technology than long-range missiles. In the real world, defending against 5–20 warheads may be no more realistic than Reagan's dream of building an impenetrable shield.

NATIONAL MISSILE DEFENSES STILL THREATEN DEEP REDUCTIONS IN NUCLEAR WEAPONS

More than fifteen years after Reagan's Star Wars speech, there are still compelling security reasons not to build a national missile defense. The most effective way to reduce the nuclear threat to the United States is to make deep reductions in nuclear arsenals worldwide, and the end of the cold war now makes this feasible. However, such deep cuts will almost certainly be derailed by U.S. deployment of a national missile defense, because missile defenses can more easily threaten a small deterrent force than a large one. Perversely, even though a missile defense is unlikely to be very effective, other countries are likely to assume it would be and will act accordingly by resisting deep reductions.

Indeed, Russia has made it clear that it remains concerned about U.S. missile defenses and that its continued compliance with nuclear reductions under the START agreements depends on continued U.S. compliance with the 1972 Anti-Ballistic Missile (ABM) Treaty, which prohibits national missile defenses. Moreover, given the ongoing attempts by some Congressional members to mandate the deployment of national missile defenses, Russia would likely (and not unreasonably) see deployment of even a limited system as the first installment of a larger system.

> "To the extent complete prevention [of a weapons of mass destruction attack] is impossible, being prepared to respond efficiently... to such an attack and reducing its effects becomes crucial."

EMERGENCY RESPONSE TEAMS CAN MITIGATE THE EFFECTS OF A CHEMICAL OR BIOLOGICAL ATTACK

Frank J. Cilluffo and Jack Thomas Tomarchio

In response to the threat of chemical or biological terrorism, U.S. government agencies have taken a number of steps toward bolstering emergency preparedness. Frank J. Cilluffo and Jack Thomas Tomarchio assert in the following viewpoint that locally based emergency response teams can help lessen the negative consequences of a chemical or biological attack. Cilluffo is a senior analyst at the Washington, D.C. Center for Strategic and International Studies, a nonpartisan public policy institution dedicated to policy analysis. Tomarchio is general counsel of Aloe Investment Corporation in Wayne, Pennsylvania. He is also a lieutenant colonel in the U.S. Army Reserves.

As you read, consider the following questions:

1. According to Cilluffo and Tomarchio, in what ways has the potential for terrorism increased?
2. In the authors' opinion, why are emergency response capabilities essential to preparing for a chemical or biological attack?

Excerpted from Frank J. Cilluffo and Jack Thomas Tomarchio, "Responding to New Terrorist Threats," Orbis, Summer 1998. Footnotes in the original have been omitted in this reprint. Reprinted by permission of JAI Press.

The terrorist cell was formed in 1996. Never exceeding more than six members, the cell had worked quietly and with efficient determination. During the months prior to going operational, targeting data had been painstakingly acquired, escape routes chosen, traffic patterns analyzed, weather and atmospheric conditions studied. Money needed to fund the operation was carefully laundered so that it became untraceable. Much of it was actually raised under the guise of relief organizations here in the United States. The operation had been rehearsed, refined, and re-rehearsed until it could be executed with split-second alacrity. Logistical hurdles had been surmounted and the deadly weapons needed to accomplish the mission were in place. The target, a mid-sized American city of just over 200,000, had never known terrorism before. Most of its citizens had never heard the exotic sounding names of the biological and chemical agents that would soon kill them.

The operation called for the activation of the weapons at three different sites within the city limits. The sites were carefully chosen for their population density, vehicular traffic congestion, and distance from each other. At the prearranged time the weapons are detonated. The first three explode within minutes of each other while a second series of blasts is intentionally timed to detonate only after police and fire units arrive at the scene of the initial attacks, thus making them immediate victims of the terrorist onslaught. Unseen amid the growing carnage, small canisters of biological toxins are electronically opened at several more sites in the city, releasing microscopic payloads into the atmosphere.

Simultaneously, but thousands of miles away, malicious code, not unlike a computer virus, is surreptitiously inserted through the public switching network, virtually crippling the city's phone system, including its 911 service. It also has the cascading effect of overloading police and fire communications frequencies.

A PARALYZING ATTACK

The resulting carnage is horrific. Within minutes the chemicals have sown death over a ten square block swath of the city's business district. The university, three miles from the city's hub, is also paralyzed by the attack. And in the densely populated housing projects in the northeast quadrant of town, thousands are already dead. Police and fire assets are quickly overwhelmed. Isolated from each other amid the concerted chaos that has now seized the city, and unable to communicate over their emergency radio bands, the rescue personnel are rendered powerless to confront the holocaust around them. Victims now pour towards hospitals which are ill equipped and have limited supplies of antidotes to treat their symptoms. Unless they have been decontaminated prior to arriving at the hospital most find the doors to medical treatment shut, as hospitals fear exposing patients and health care workers to the unknown toxin.

Two days later, thousands more begin to die as the delayed effects of the biologicals—the silent killer—are at last apparent. The initial casualties are now compounded many fold, as the symptoms begin to manifest themselves.

The effect upon the city is devastating—tens of thousands of corpses and dozens of city blocks contaminated—but the impact upon the country is even greater, for this disaster marks the first successful use of weapons of mass destruction (WMD) in the United States. The political aftershocks are of seismic proportions as the nation's trust and confidence in its government is shaken to the bedrock. Equally alarming is the seeming ease with which the attack was accomplished and the total inability of emergency personnel to manage the crisis. America is exposed as defenseless. It cannot even retaliate.

THE NEW TERRORISTS

The above scenario, though fictional, is one that keeps federal, state, and local officials awake at night. Often euphemistically referred to as the "worst-case scenario," the potential for terrorism on American soil is generating heightened interest, especially in light of the aborted plot to bomb the New York City subway system, the February 1998 arrest of two men charged with conspiring to possess the biological agent Bacillus anthracis for use as a weapon, the 1995 bombing of the Alfred P. Murrah Federal Building in Oklahoma City, the 1993 attack on the World Trade Center, and the foiled 1992 attempt in Minnesota by members of an antigovernment tax group, the Minnesota Patriots, to kill government officials by using the deadly toxin ricin, a powdered protein extract of common castor beans, all of which were intended to cause a maximum number of casualties. From 1992 to 1998 at least eleven states have experienced terrorist incidents.

The face of terrorism is changing and so are its methods. A new breed of terrorists is seeking out and using weapons of greater lethality that can affect scores of victims over large areas. For conspirators hoping, or at least willing, to inflict mass casualties, nuclear, chemical, and biological weapons are the tools of choice in their arsenal. With the tremendous impact that the use of these weapons carry, the terrorist target often becomes not those actually killed but the millions watching CNN and the nightly news at home.

Nor do these terrorists represent only the traditional zealots promoting national liberation or ethnic self-determination. Rather, the terrorist brew has been fortified by single-issue extremists, cults, religious fanatics, and insurgent reactionaries. Such second-generation terrorists are motivated by vengeance, rage, racial or religious hatred, intense antigovernment feelings, or extreme nationalism. Their agendas differ markedly from their classical terrorist counterparts in that they are not seeking a seat at the negotiating table. They want to blow up the table altogether and build a new one in its place. . . .

REDUCING VULNERABILITY TO TERRORISM

Reducing American vulnerability to terrorism is an exceedingly complex and multifaceted process that must incorporate means of prevention, deterrence, preemption, and crisis and consequence management. On November 14, 1994, in recognition of the threat that WMD terrorism poses to our national security, President Clinton issued Executive Order 12938, "Proliferation of Weapons of Mass Destruction," in which he declared a national emergency to deal with the threat.

In June 1995, Clinton promulgated Presidential Decision Directive 39 (PDD-39), which established U.S. policy on deterring, defeating, and responding to terrorism, including WMD. Under PDD-39, the National Security Council is responsible for coordinating interagency counterterrorism policy and reviewing ongoing crisis operations. It also spells out agency roles and missions and indicates that the State Department is the lead agency overseas and the FBI within the continental United States. The Federal Emergency Management Agency (FEMA), in turn, has the lead with respect to consequence management, including the terrorist use of nuclear, chemical, and biological weapons.

With respect to WMD, federal agencies under the leadership of the Departments of Defense (DOD), Energy, and State, together with the FBI and CIA, have worked diligently to monitor the proliferation of WMD and potential customers of such weapons and materials. Detection of and protection against a WMD attack are particularly difficult tasks, however, since many substances needed to produce such weapons, especially chemical and biological ones (for which no infrastructure is needed), are easily obtained or produced. Likewise, there are multiple methods of delivery or dissemination available, but few signatures from which to provide early warning.

THE ROLE OF INTELLIGENCE

A more robust use of intelligence assets is needed today to prevent and repel terrorist activities. While any success entails all-source intelligence collection, and maintaining a substantial technical intelligence base is important, it is critical that the United States augment human intelligence (HUMINT) capability, since only human sources can provide timely indications and threat warnings regarding future plans such as target selection and weaponry. Moreover, HUMINT must be used in a highly innovative manner in order to penetrate these "hard" targets and acquire the "right" sources within the decision-making loop of terrorist organizations.

Unfortunately, no matter how vigilant we are in our efforts to detect WMD and preempt those who would use them, the success rate can never reach 100 percent. The sad truth is that the determined terrorist, especially one who is prepared to accept his own destruction in the course of a terrorist act, is exceedingly hard to frustrate.

CONSEQUENCE MANAGEMENT

One way in which federal and state officials can make an immediate impact upon the terrorist threat is in the area of consequence management, by mitigating the deadly effects of such acts. As the above scenario illustrates, state and local emergency response capabilities, and the first responders themselves, are inherently vulnerable to a well-planned WMD attack. The situation is simply exacerbated when information warfare is used as a force multiplier to disrupt emergency communications and hinder civil response during a terrorist attack.

The challenge then is to empower our states and municipalities to minimize the effects of a terrorist attack by training our police, fire, and emergency medical personnel in such areas as WMD agent identification and detection, on-site decontamination, crowd control, symptom recognition, medical triage and initial treatment of casualties, handling of the deceased, safe transport of victims, media relations, and emergency communications. The federal government, recognizing the importance of consequence management, funded a $52.6 million domestic preparedness program in fiscal year (FY) 1997 in 120 U.S. cities.

In preparation for the G-7 meeting at Denver, that city was logically selected for such a pilot program that began in January

1998, with New York, Los Angeles, Chicago, Houston, the District of Columbia, Philadelphia, San Diego, and Kansas City to begin their training in FY 1997. By the end of 1999, a total of 120 cities should have received training and assistance from the federal government. Using instructors from the army, the Department of Energy, the Environmental Protection Agency, FEMA, and the FBI, the aim of the program is to train first-responders to manage a chemical, nuclear, or biological attack. In doing so, the Departments of Defense and Energy are expanding on existing capabilities present in the Marine Corps' Chemical and Biological Incident Response Force (CBIRF), the army's Technical Escort Unit (TEU), and the Energy Department's Nuclear Emergency Search Team (NEST). These units, however, are small and cannot provide the rapid response capability that is needed should a WMD be used against a population center in the United States. Often based in remote locations, they may need as much as six to twelve hours to deploy to the site of a terrorist act.

During the so-called "golden hour," the clinically relevant window of opportunity in which initial medical treatment must be administered in order to turn victims into patients, emergency response personnel must be prepared for immediate action. But with the exception of fire fighters, emergency medical technicians, and police, there are no other first responders who can be mobilized during that critical time. In any case, few, if any, of these personnel have the equipment, resources, and training they need to respond effectively to WMD. Thus, the initiatives currently launched to assist in major disasters, including those of the National Defense Medical System and Disaster Medical Assistance Teams, must be augmented with well-trained and disciplined local units who, because of their geographical location, can respond quickly to an emergency.

MOBILIZING FIRST RESPONDERS

Fortunately, such forces potentially exist today, and in all fifty states—the National Guard and reserves. Numbering over 910,000 persons, these forces are already trained in combat and combat support roles that mirror many of the capabilities of their active duty counterparts.

Using National Guard and reserve forces to counter the effects of terrorist acts would permit these units to recalibrate their training from a regimen that stressed the old superpower rivalry to one that recognizes the contemporary environment in which asymmetric terrorist tactics may be employed by adver-

FEDERAL RESPONSE UNITS FOR INCIDENTS INVOLVING WEAPONS OF MASS DESTRUCTION

	Agency	Background
Domestic Emergency Support Team (DEST)	FBI-managed interagency team	Activated in 1995 to provide expert advice to domestic agencies responsible for managing weapons of mass destruction incidents.
Federal Emergency Support Team (FEST)	Department of State	Activated in 1986 to manage foreign incidents involving weapons of mass destruction.
Nuclear Emergency Support Team (NEST)	Department of Energy	Activated in 1974 to provide technical assistance to the FBI on nuclear incidents. Fields mobile search teams to locate radiological devices.
Metropolitan Medical Strike Teams (MMST)	Department of Health and Human Services	Prototype teams established in 1996 to provide on-site response and transport of patients to hospital emergency rooms. Intended to cover 100 cities.
Chemical Biological Incident Response Force (CBIRF)	Marine Corps	Activated in April 1996 and based in Camp Lejeune, North Carolina, to treat and evaluate casualties, and provide local security, detection, and decontamination.
Technical Escort Unit (TEU)	Army	Origins from World War II; provides response worldwide for escorting and disposing chemical and biological weapons.
Rapid Assessment and Initial Detection Teams (RAID)	National Guard	To provide rapid assessment of biological and chemical incidents, and supply initial detection equipment. Ten teams to be stationed in areas determined by the Federal Emergency Management Agency.

James H. Anderson, *Heritage Foundation Backgrounder*, May 26, 1998.

saries seeking to level the playing field with the United States. In the case of the National Guard this new mission would, ironically, mean a return to its historical role as a militia force empowered to safeguard and maintain public safety at home. . . .

Guard and reserve units based in close proximity to virtually every major metropolitan area in the United States could swiftly and easily arrive at any crisis area in the nation. With time of the essence in a terrorist scenario, the speed of the first responders is of critical concern to emergency planners. Having pre-positioned forces from the National Guard and reserves available for quick mobilization in the event of a terrorist attack ensures that no part of the country is without coverage. Certainly the deterrent effect of having such highly trained forces dispersed throughout the nation and dedicated to the detection of WMD and management of a WMD incident would be not lost on potential terrorists.

WHAT IS TO BE DONE

Enhancing our ability to respond to a WMD incident by using National Guard and reserve forces would require several changes in the way we think about national security and emergency preparedness.

First, the training that is now being given to police and fire departments in 120 U.S. cities should be offered to selected units in the guard and reserves. This can be initially accomplished by selecting one state as a pilot location. Selection criteria should include a state with well-defined pockets of urban population, a state having large and well-trained National Guard and reserve units, and optimally a state that will be agreeable to shouldering some of the cost of the training.

Secondly, coordination among the Departments of Defense and Justice, FEMA, the Public Health Service, the intelligence community, and other federal agencies is critical to design an effective training program that can be implemented in the reserves and National Guard. With the passage of Public Law 104-201, *The Defense Against Weapons of Mass Destruction Act*, the DOD has been designated as the lead agency for domestic preparedness against WMD. Within the DOD, the Office of the Secretary of Defense for Special Operations and Low Intensity Conflict (OSD/SOLIC) is responsible for supervisory oversight. The assistant secretary of defense provides resource oversight for actual equipment procurement and the secretary of the army is designated the executive agent responsible for planning, implementation, and procedures. The secretary of the army, subsequently named the director of military support of the army staff, as the

DOD staff action agent, and the army's Chemical/Biological Defense Command are responsible for actually implementing the program. These offices now need to take a hard look at the feasibility of integrating the National Guard and reserves into the crisis response and consequence management portions of the defense from WMD program.

Thirdly, procurement of specialized detection and decontamination kits, currently designed for and used by active units, must be made available to the National Guard and reserves. These would include sophisticated computer and communications equipment, detection kits, personal protective suits, sensors, decontamination tents, and specialized medical equipment and antidotes adapted for biological, chemical, and radiological casualties.

Fourthly, a mentoring program must be established between the National Guard, the reserves, and those elements in the federal law-enforcement and intelligence communities responsible for antiterrorism programs. The skills contained in the Marine Corps' excellent CBIRF program, for example, now need to be extended to select National Guard and reserve units. Once sufficient National Guard and reserve training cadres have been established, these trainers can begin the important process of training others in the various state units. Nothing less than a seamless integration between the National Guard and reserves and the various intelligence, law-enforcement, and operational communities now responsible for anti-terrorism must be achieved. . . .

KEYS TO SUCCESS

A terrorist attack involving WMD, no matter what the source, would have catastrophic effects on American society beyond the deaths it might cause. As such, we cannot afford a major incident. Preventing and deterring groups from engaging in such activities must be a national priority. But to the extent complete prevention is impossible, being prepared to respond efficiently and seamlessly to such an attack and reducing its effects becomes crucial. Given its unique capabilities, assets, and experience, the DOD must assume the leadership role in preventing, deterring, compelling, and responding to WMD terror within the continental United States. The keys to success are continued leadership as a policy priority and sustained funding through the out-years to ensure that all agencies, local, state, regional, and federal, are sufficiently equipped, trained, exercised, and prepared to respond effectively to a WMD attack. It is in the nation's interest that the Pentagon remain the executive agent for the domestic preparedness program in WMD defense, hence its mandate must be extended beyond FY 1999, as initially required by the Defense Authorization Bill.

The fuse on a major terrorist event in the United States may already be lit, in which case it is no longer a matter of whether, but when and where an incident occurs. The federal government, elected representatives, and state and local government officials should begin a concerted effort now to enhance our national security by maximizing the unique abilities within the National Guard and reserves to safeguard our nation from WMD terrorism.

"Early [medical] detection of a
bioterror event not only would save
lives, it also would enable law
enforcement people to get on the
trail of a terrorist faster."

A STRONG PUBLIC HEALTH SYSTEM CAN MANAGE THE CONSEQUENCES OF A BIOLOGICAL ATTACK

Richard Preston

In the following viewpoint, Richard Preston argues that improvements to the public health system could help alleviate the consequences of a biological attack. In order to prepare for such an attack, claims Preston, doctors must be trained to diagnose the diseases caused by biological weapons, and antidotes to these diseases must be stockpiled. Preston is the author of *The Cobra Event*, a fictional account of a biological attack, and *The Hot Zone*, a nonfiction book that chronicles the outbreak of Ebola in Africa.

As you read, consider the following questions:

1. According to Preston, what would happen if anthrax were released into the air of New York City?
2. What steps should be taken to educate health care workers about biological weapons, in the author's view?
3. Why, in Preston's opinion, is smallpox the most dangerous biological weapon?

For decades, the conventional view among American scientists was that biological weapons aren't much of a problem. Meanwhile, powerful bioweapons were developed and deployed by the Soviet Union and probably by other countries, and the knowledge of how to make them has spread. Smallpox virus can be made in glass jars the size of wine bottles and released into the air with a humidifier. One F.B.I. scientist said to me: "We're seeing a lot of hoaxes, and incompetent people trying to make biological weapons. The incidents are happening at a rate of roughly one a month. My feeling is that sooner or later someone is going to get it right."

Having failed to identify the problem or come to grips with it intellectually or technically, the scientific community and the Government now owe the public a makeup effort. It could start with a few simple measures that would make us safer and less vulnerable.

INVOLVING PUBLIC HEALTH DOCTORS

As experts with whom I've been talking see it, the first step needs to be the involvement of public health doctors in emergency planning. Yet the Centers for Disease Control and Prevention remains largely uninvolved, disconnected from the planning loop and inadequately financed for the task. State and local public health surveillance needs to be strengthened. That would have an immediate payoff, since it would help control new and emerging "natural" diseases that are now taking lives in this country. And if a bioterror attack is recognized early, many lives can be saved.

Consider what might actually happen if a pound or two of dried anthrax were released into the air of New York City. Many thousands of people might be exposed, but only a small fraction of them would get sick and die. It would happen over time—time enough to save many people if some basic preparations have been made.

THE CASE OF ANTHRAX

Anthrax incubates silently in the body for three days to several weeks after exposure. Then the first symptoms appear. Virtually no doctor in the United States has seen a case of anthrax or knows how to diagnose it. The symptoms of anthrax resemble flu or a cold; then the victim dies of what looks like pneumonia. Many days might pass before it would finally become apparent that New York had been hit with anthrax. But where? And how much anthrax went into the air? The F.B.I. would come under excruciating pressure to find the perpetrator, who would be long gone, and the trail might have gone cold.

Everyone in the city would wonder if he had been exposed and whether another attack might occur. There would be an overwhelming demand for antibiotics, which can cure anthrax provided they are taken before symptoms appear. Antibiotics would disappear from the shelves instantly, and the demand would create a national shortage.

THE HEALTH CARE SYSTEM IS UNPREPARED

In February of 1998, police officers arrested two men in Las Vegas, Nevada, on suspicion of possessing anthrax. FBI teams from Washington, D.C., and army units from Utah scrambled in. "Everything worked the way it should have worked," FBI director Louis Freeh later told Congress. But with no capable testing facilities nearby, agents had to fly the sample all the way back to Washington aboard an FBI jet and then on a helicopter to an army lab in Maryland. Anxious officials had to wait 30 hours to find out that the powder was not deadly anthrax but a vaccine.

Despite the rapid response, the episode exposed one of the biggest holes in the safety net: the weakness of the medical system. Only a handful of laboratories can identify exotic diseases like bubonic plague, anthrax, or smallpox—causing delays that may cost countless lives. Only one of the Domestic Preparedness Program's courses focuses on health care workers. Stores of vaccines, antibiotics, and antidotes are pitifully inadequate. The United States has only about 7 million doses of smallpox vaccine—an amount that would vanish overnight in a major epidemic. More vaccines alone, though, are not sufficient. . . .

"We have no plans for mass casualties," Dr. Michael Osterholm explains. "If we suddenly see thousands and thousands of people dying from this, like every other community in the country, we'd have to start renting freezer trucks for bodies."

Kermit Pattison, *George*, July 1998.

There is a good vaccine for anthrax. It can work even if it's given to a person who has already been exposed. The Government would need to fly in many tons of antibiotics and vaccine. But there's no stockpile of antibiotics or anthrax vaccine. Such a stockpile could stop the dying quickly and reduce fear. It might also discourage a terrorist from using anthrax.

EDUCATING HEALTH CARE WORKERS

A Web site should be set up that any public-health or primary-care doctor could look at, offering basic information and training modules in anthrax and smallpox. (Wannabe terrorists are already using the Internet to spread information about bioweapons; they're ahead of the public-health doctors.) A medical training module would cost around $200,000 to set up: peanuts. Yet it could make a big difference. Early detection of a bioterror event not only would save lives, it also would enable law enforcement people to get on the trail of a terrorist faster.

Anthrax isn't contagious and doesn't spread. Smallpox spreads like chain lightning, and since the entire human species now lacks immunity to smallpox (the shot wears off), it is the planet's most dangerous potential biological weapon. If smallpox were released anywhere in this country, experts believe that at least 20 million to 30 million people would need to be vaccinated quickly to stop the surging outbreak. Right now, there are only about seven million usable doses of vaccine on hand.

STOCKING UP ON VACCINES

There is a new way to make smallpox vaccine that is fast and cheap. But it needs approval from the Food and Drug Administration, and manufacturing capability must be set up. Enough vaccine to protect the entire American population could be stored in a building smaller than a garage, and the vaccine would last for decades before it had to be replaced with fresh stocks. That would pretty much remove smallpox from the arsenal of a terrorist. It would also take smallpox away from Saddam Hussein far more effectively (and cheaply) than bombing his laboratories.

One other step is needed. The community of biologists in the United States has maintained a kind of hand-wringing silence on the ethics of creating bioweapons—a reluctance to talk about it with the public, even a disbelief that it's happening. Biological weapons are a disgrace to biology. The time has come for top biologists to assert their leadership and speak out, to take responsibility on behalf of their profession for the existence of these weapons and the means of protecting the population against them, just as leading physicists did a generation ago when nuclear weapons came along. Moral pressure costs nothing and can help; silence is unacceptable now.

> "[The Cooperative Threat Reduction program] ... is directly responsible for removing 4,000 warheads from operational status in [the former Soviet Union]."

SAFEGUARDING RUSSIAN NUCLEAR STOCKPILES WILL PREVENT A NUCLEAR ATTACK

Richard Lugar

The collapse of the Soviet Union led to a decrease in the security of nuclear storage facilities in that area. As a result, some fear that nuclear weapons material is easily accessible to terrorists. Richard Lugar, a U.S. Senator from Indiana, contends in the following viewpoint that through the Cooperative Threat Reduction program, the United States can reduce the risk of nuclear terrorism by helping Russia secure its nuclear storage facilities and dismantle its nuclear warheads.

As you read, consider the following questions:

1. According to Lugar, how has the collapse of the Soviet Union made weapons of mass destruction more accessible?
2. What steps can be taken to prevent the smuggling of Russian nuclear weapons material, in the author's view?
3. How does the Nunn-Lugar-Domenici legislation reduce the threat of nuclear terrorism, in Lugar's opinion?

Abridged from Richard Lugar, "Clear and Present Danger: Crafting a Response to Nuclear Anarchy," *Harvard International Review*, Fall 1996. Reprinted by permission of the *Harvard International Review*.

The first act of nuclear terrorism in the post-Cold War era occurred in November 1995 when Chechen rebels placed a package of radioactive material in a Moscow park. Chechen separatists took credit for placing a 30-pound box containing small amounts of cesium-137, a radioactive material that causes cancer and other severe health problems when it comes into contact with human skin, at the entrance of the park. While the container was not equipped with explosives necessary to disperse the cesium, this incident is illustrative of the danger posed by the nuclear materials that continue to steal in and out of Russia and the other states that make up the former Soviet Union.

In several incidents, beginning in 1992, highly enriched uranium was seized in sting operations across Russia and Eastern Europe. In one such case, a captain in the Russian Navy stole ten pounds of highly enriched uranium from a submarine storage facility. In another case, an employee of a nuclear laboratory stole 3.7 pounds of highly enriched uranium from his employer.

The most terrifying aspect of the seizures is that in each incident the intended final destination of the hazardous material remains unknown. Perhaps it was en route to the states or organizations of the Persian Gulf like Iraq, Iran, or Hamas, or it could have been going to a right-wing militant group in the United States. Any of these possibilities is worrisome. Such groups do not hesitate to unleash death and destruction upon the population and the cities of the United States. The bombings at the Atlanta Olympics, in Oklahoma City, and at the World Trade Center pale in comparison to the devastation which could have been wrought had the explosive devices used been nuclear, biological, or chemical.

A Supermarket of Dangerous Weapons

When the Soviet Union collapsed, a potential supermarket of nuclear, biological, and chemical (NBC) weapons and material became increasingly accessible. Vast quantities of weapons and weapons-usable material remain at hundreds of Russian sites. At each of these sites, the people charged with assuring the security of these valuable materials are struggling to feed themselves and their families. At many facilities, personnel can enter and leave without passing any electronic detection or alarm system. The decay of the custodial system guarding the Soviet nuclear legacy has eliminated this key nuclear proliferation checkpoint. Various states and terrorist groups can now buy or steal what they previously had to produce on their own.

In the years since the collapse of the Soviet Union, there have been hundreds of attempts to smuggle nuclear materials. The German government has reported more than 700 cases of attempted nuclear sales between 1991 and 1994. One Russian report states that in 1993 there were 11 attempted thefts of uranium, some 900 attempts at illegal entry at nuclear facilities, and nearly 700 instances in which workers at nuclear sites tried to steal secret documents.

These facts are grounds for grave concern. The large number of attempts to sell nuclear, biological, or chemical materials suggests a widespread appreciation within Russia that these materials have market value. Indeed, there is a considerable effort within Russia to fill the supply side of an emerging international NBC black market. In addition, the numerous failed attempts to move nuclear materials across international borders are less important than the reality that even a tiny number of successes in transferring nuclear weapons or material could produce disastrous consequences. Moreover, it is unlikely that every attempt at nuclear smuggling is detected and reported; by definition, successful transactions on black markets are covert and thus go unnoticed. Finally, and perhaps most importantly, among the large number of claimed cases, there are a small number of serious, unchallenged, and unambiguously dangerous incidents.

Although the likelihood of an all-out nuclear war has declined with the end of the Cold War, the risk of nuclear detonation in the United States will increase if terrorists gain access to Russian nuclear stockpiles. If the United States fails to produce a response to an NBC leakage which would be as focused, serious, and vigorous as its Cold War strategy, Americans have every reason to anticipate acts of nuclear, chemical, or biological terrorism against U.S. targets before this decade is over.

SECURING WEAPONS MATERIAL

The first priority of a comprehensive program to meet this threat must be to ensure that all NBC weapons and weapons-usable materials are secure and accounted for. The United States must therefore help modernize security and accounting systems at all former Soviet facilities, establish a national accounting system, and improve transport security. Other near-term objectives must include continued consolidation of material storage sites, as well as mass production of modern material protection, control, and accounting (MPC&A) equipment in Russia.

If MPC&A systems fail and nuclear material is stolen, anti-smuggling efforts must form an important second line of defense. Increased police and intelligence training and cooperation across borders must be top priorities. This is a global problem that requires international cooperation, and it is in the interests of all nations that are not attempting to acquire weapons material and know-how to cooperate. At the least, we can expect the NATO nations, NATO hopefuls, and the nations of the former Soviet Union to join in these efforts.

The United States must work to reach agreement with Russia on a broad, reciprocal regime on management and disposal of excess uranium and plutonium. This regime should include declarations of stockpiles of all NBC weapons and materials, followed by cooperative measures that would clarify and confirm those declarations. The final goal would be a monitored halt to the production of materials and agreed net reductions from these stockpiles.

The United States has agreed to purchase excess highly enriched uranium (HEU) from Russia. In turn, Russia has indicated informally that it has substantially more HEU that it would be willing to sell. Additional purchases would help reduce stockpiles in Russia, create further incentives for warhead dismantlement, and provide much-needed hard currency to Russia. Acceleration of these purchases would reduce the time the material remained in weapons-usable form. Arrangements might also be made under which the profits from the additional U.S. purchases would be used by Russia to fund other nuclear security objectives.

A successful program must also work to develop and diversify the economic base of the nuclear cities in the former Soviet Union. Economic collapse in these cities would pose a serious threat to security, given the large quantities of nuclear weapons and materials stored there. As long as these cities have no new mission, they will continue to lobby energetically for the continued production of nuclear weapons and materials. Thus, helping to diversify the economic base of these cities must be a fundamental part of achieving U.S. and international security objectives over the long term. The United States is already helping to achieve these objectives through the Industrial Partnership Program, which employs scientists and engineers in peaceful applications of technology in projects cost-shared by U.S. industry.

THE COOPERATIVE THREAT REDUCTION PROGRAM

The original Cooperative Threat Reduction program, cosponsored by Senator Sam Nunn (D-GA) and myself, passed Congress in 1991 and was the first step toward addressing the need for protection against the nuclear threat. Over time, Nunn-Lugar, as it came to be called, has authorized more than $1.5 billion for denuclearization in the former Soviet Union and is directly responsible for removing over 4,000 warheads from operational status in that area. Kazakhstan and the Ukraine became totally nuclear-free in 1995, and Belarus is expected to follow. Decreasing the number of nuclear states in the world by three in just five years is surely one of the great successes of the modern era.

NEW SECURITY MEASURES

The Department of Energy is installing advanced U.S. material protection technology to increase [the] security [of Russian nuclear materials] at sensitive sites in conjunction with the Russian Federation. Physical protection devices, such as motion detectors, cameras, and vibration sensors have been placed in rooms containing weapons-grade material. Vibration sensors, placed on doors and walls, are necessary to prevent a determined thief from breaking into a room using a drill or heavy-duty saw. Doors and windows were hardened to delay intruders, and sensors and cameras were added to thwart theft or diversion of nuclear materials. At the Beloyarsk Nuclear Power Plant (BNPP) in Zarechny, a vehicle and personnel portal were upgraded to include a motorized vehicle gate and a vehicle entrapment area. The response force at BNPP and Sverdlovsk Branch of the Research and Development Institute of Power Engineering (SF-NIKIET) received upgraded radio communication equipment that allows them to communicate and respond more effectively.

United States Department of Energy, M2 Presswire, April 28, 1998.

However, there is a serious lack of domestic security against the threat posed by the proliferation of nuclear weapons and materials. Terrorism experts and local officials uniformly agree that our cities and towns simply are not equipped to deal with a chemical, biological, or nuclear incident.

In the summer of 1996, Senator Nunn and I were joined by Senator Pete Domenici (R-NM) in drafting legislation that will take nuclear threat reduction a step further. The Nunn-Lugar-Domenici initiative focuses on controlling not only nuclear, chemical, and biological weapons, but also the proliferation of the materials and technology necessary to construct such weapons. The legislation aims at enhancing the preparedness of emergency management teams as well as fire and police departments in U.S. cities and towns to respond to emergencies involving the threat or use of weapons of mass destruction. The bill is also concerned with upgrading the security of borders in the former Soviet Union and in the United States, as well as the security controls at the source of much of the material.

RESPONDING TO AN ATTACK

To enhance our ability to respond to nuclear, chemical, and biological incidents on U.S. soil, the legislation calls for training, equipping, and improving coordination among the appropriate federal, state, and local officials. A new position of national Coordinator will be created to further improve overall coordination of U.S. government policy regarding the causes and effects of proliferation. The Coordinator, reporting directly to the President, will be responsible for making recommendations for ensuring appropriate cooperation and coordination within and among federal, state, and local governments, combatting proliferation, and integrating agency budgets.

The other component of the legislation improves the U.S. government's ability to interdict the transit of weapons of mass destruction and related materials by bolstering the U.S. Customs Service and by recommending an increase in penalties for crimes associated with the proliferation of these weapons and materials. To limit the threat from abroad, the legislation increases programs in the original Nunn-Lugar program which have proven most necessary and most effective. These provisions aim at either speeding up the destruction of or improving the controls and safeguards over weapons of mass destruction and related materials and technologies throughout the former Soviet Union.

In July 1996, Nunn-Lugar II was introduced in the U.S. Senate as an amendment to the Defense Authorization bill and passed 96-0. The Senate voted 100-0 to appropriate the funds necessary to implement the Nunn-Lugar-Domenici Amendment. Following negotiations with the House, the program was fully authorized in the conference report to the fiscal year 1997 National Defense Authorization Act.

Despite this apparent success, the program has come under attack by some in the media and in the House of Representatives. Some critics of the program argue that the threat of nuclear terrorism is exaggerated and that the funding for the program—often improperly characterized as foreign aid rather than U.S. defense—is excessive in a time of tight fiscal policy. Even limited programs under the Cooperative Threat Reduction Act and the Department of Energy's lab-to-lab program to assist Russia in securing these materials have been attacked on the Hill as not representing legitimate defense needs. It sometimes seems that it will take the detonation of a nuclear, chemical, or biological device on U.S. soil to develop a realistic appreciation for the magnitude of this problem and the real threat to U.S. security.

In their 1996 book *Avoiding Nuclear Anarchy*, Graham Allison, Owen Cote, Jr., Richard Falkenrath, and Steve Miller note that, "more fissionable material is now stored in improvised, insecure facilities at Sverdlovsk [a city in the former Soviet Union] than is contained in the entire stockpiles of Britain, France and China combined. Even if 99.99 percent of Russia's fissile material stocks remained secure, but the other .01 percent leaked, more than 10 North Korea's worth of fissile materials would be loose and no one would know." A nuclear explosion can be created with as little as 2.2 pounds of plutonium or 5.5 pounds of highly enriched uranium.

Furthermore, there is a small but dangerous and highly motivated group of aspiring proliferators—including Iran, Iraq, and North Korea—which have made strenuous efforts to obtain fissile materials, and their successful access to Russian stockpiles is not an impossibility. A group of Russian nuclear experts was arrested shortly before their plane was set to take off for North Korea, where they had been hired to work on the nuclear program. Iran is reported to have sent "buying teams" into the former Soviet Union for its nuclear weapons program. For a Russian engineer, guard, or scientist, the opportunity to steal and sell a cache of fissile material could well be irresistible.

MEETING THE CHALLENGE OF TERRORISM

NBC weapons in the hands of extremists willing to use them would produce terrorism of an unprecedented magnitude. Beyond terrorism, if significant amounts of nuclear material flow from Russia, they could make the development of nuclear weapons much easier for states that have found bomb programs too expensive and technically beyond their capabilities. Although the ultimate terror would be a working bomb constructed by terrorists on their own, the much likelier catastrophe is a large purchase of plutonium by a country looking for a shortcut to a nuclear arsenal.

This direct threat to U.S. security requires a fully formulated and funded immediate action. . . . In order to meet the nuclear challenge, it is important that the President, the Congress, and all U.S. citizens appreciate the magnitude of the problem and act to circumscribe this threat to the U.S. security before a nuclear device is detonated on U.S. soil.

> "[The Nuclear Emergency Search Team] has evaluated 110 [nuclear] threats, and mobilized itself to deal with about 30 of them."

NUCLEAR DETECTION TEAMS CAN AVERT A SURPRISE ATTACK

Douglas Waller

The Nuclear Emergency Search Team (NEST), established in 1975 by the Department of Energy, provides technical assistance to the FBI in the event of a terrorist threat involving nuclear weapons. Members of NEST are trained to detect radioactive material and dismantle nuclear weapons. In the following viewpoint, Douglas Waller maintains that NEST has helped expose fraudulent nuclear threats and is prepared to deal with real incidents of nuclear terrorism. Waller writes for *Time* magazine.

As you read, consider the following questions:

1. According to Waller, what steps does NEST take to locate a nuclear bomb?
2. Why are radiation detectors difficult to operate, according to the author?
3. What methods could NEST use to dismantle a nuclear device, in Waller's view?

It might be hard to picture at this juncture in American history, but there are times, even now, when working for the government can be exciting. Consider a secret Department of Energy training exercise—code name: Mirage Gold—that was staged in New Orleans in October 1994. Hundreds of normally lab-bound nuclear scientists fanned out through the French Quarter carrying briefcases with hidden radiation detectors, while rental vans packed with high-tech electronics roamed the streets and planes fitted with spy cameras swooped overhead. After three days, they found what they were hunting for: a simulated nuclear weapon hidden on a nearby naval base.

There is more to these games than merely giving government employees the chance to play James Bond. The point is to test the preparedness of a secretive task force organized to combat the possibility—eventuality, some would say—of nuclear terrorism in the U.S. Welcome to Fail Safe, the post–cold war edition.

Until now, and hopefully for a long time to come, the spectacle of the U.S. government being blackmailed by nuclear terrorists has been the province of books, movies (including a John Travolta film) and a series of scary, attention-getting commercials by attention-needing 1996 presidential candidate Richard Lugar. Of course, the appeal of nuclear weapons to terrorists is obvious: if destabilizing society or drawing attention to one's cause is the goal, a mushroom cloud outranks truck bombs and sarin attacks.

The danger is real. Making a nuclear weapon is a complex business, but in essence all anyone would need to lay waste to a medium-size city like New Orleans are two things. The first is an understanding of the technology involved, the easy availability of which has been demonstrated by innumerable high school science whiz kids. The second component is actual fissionable material—55 lbs. of enriched uranium, say, which would be enough to turn the heart of New Orleans into radioactive dust. With the increasing use of nuclear technology around the world and the destabilization of Russia, the once stringent global controls on uranium and plutonium are increasingly being subverted. U.S. intelligence officials admit that a terrorist would have no more difficulty slipping a nuclear device into the U.S. than a drug trafficker has bringing in bulk loads of cocaine.

This, however, is a good-news story—in the sense that the public is largely unaware of the lengths to which the U.S. government has already gone to combat the potential of nuclear terror. The CIA and FBI work at stopping threats before they happen, while the Energy Department focuses on responding to actual emergencies. Though the department has had its funding cut more than 9% from 1992 to 1996, it has almost doubled its budget for responding to nuclear emergencies, now at $70 million annually. The core of the effort is the Nuclear Emergency Search Team—NEST. These are the people America will call on if and when someone claims to have hidden an atom bomb in the Mall of America.

NEST was formed in 1975 after an extortionist threatened to blow up Boston with a nuclear device unless he was paid $200,000. Since then, NEST has evaluated 110 threats, and mobilized itself to deal with about 30 of them; like the Boston incident, all have been hoaxes. Yet NEST is more than a high-tech SWAT team. At the remote Pajarito site in the Los Alamos Nuclear Weapons Laboratory complex in New Mexico, 17 scientists are using technology found on the shelves of Radio Shack and the type of nuclear fuel sold on the black market to construct homemade bombs. To dismantle a makeshift device, scientists first must know the various ways in which it might be constructed; so far, the team has assembled more than a dozen.

Time has been permitted to take an inside look at the operations of NEST, which employs more than 1,000 men and women. Many are scientists who helped build America's nuclear arsenal. Others are volunteers from Energy Department offices around the country. All must be ready to spring into action at a moment's notice.

The first line of defense is made up of people like Lewis Newby, a former Navy pilot who heads a team of NEST scientists at Sandia National Laboratory in Albuquerque, New Mexico. Newby travels everywhere with a cellular phone and call-out roster for other team members; at home, a special beeper sits on his nightstand. When a nuclear threat is received, Newby and his colleagues must assess it. At Lawrence Livermore National Laboratory near San Francisco, NEST has a computer filled with thousands of pages of everything publicly written about making a nuclear weapon: newspaper clips, magazine articles, reports in scientific journals, even passages from spy novels. The computer can quickly run a cross-check to see if the extortionist knows what he is talking about or has merely lifted his blackmail note from a Tom Clancy book.

Assuming the threat sounds genuine, the team's first crucial task is to locate the bomb, which is presumably hidden. After flying in from around the country on military transport, NEST searchers divide the threatened city—the CIA and FBI assume terrorists will target an urban area in order to incur maximum casualties—into search grids. Energy Department aircraft, specially fitted with photographic equipment, are sent aloft to take shots of the city for detailed maps that can be used if intelligence sources narrow the search to a particular area or type of structure. Helicopters equipped with radiation detectors can sweep over the city as well, but a nuclear weapon gives off little telltale radiation and is nearly impossible to find from above a dense, urban area.

Most of the search must be conducted on the ground. Minivans are rented at the local airport, the backseats removed and replaced with electronic detectors that can sniff the neutrons and gamma radiation a nuclear device might emit. The vans, however, are only good for use in large open areas like parking lots and highways. To search narrow streets and buildings, as many as 100 two-person teams, dressed as inconspicuously as possible, are sent on foot patrols. One team member carries a special radiation detector designed to be hidden in briefcases, student backpacks, laptop computer bags—even beer coolers, in the case of a threat to vaporize the Super Bowl.

One of the searchers, "Becky" (she asked that her real name not be used), described how she made her rounds on a recent training exercise in a large city. A 31-year-old Energy Department employee who began training as a NEST searcher seven years ago, Becky and 10 colleagues were assigned to hunt for a simulated nuclear device in a hotel with 32 floors and 2,052 rooms.

Walking down the corridors, Becky and her male partner looked like the typical tourist couple on vacation, dressed in Bermuda shorts and T-shirts, cameras slung over their necks. But hidden in Becky's suitcase was a sophisticated sodium iodide crystal detector to sniff minute amounts of gamma radiation from as far away as another room.

Halfway down a corridor, Becky suddenly heard "the voice," an irritating robotic message transmitted from the suitcase to a wireless, button-sized beige receiver in her ear. "Gamma alarm four," the voice droned. That was a strong radiation signal. She glanced left at the room number on the next door and subtracted three from it. The detector's microcomputer takes several seconds to analyze the radiation and calculate its strength, so the room three doors behind her must have been the one actually giving off gamma rays.

Becky and her partner never turned around or slowed their pace, lest they attract attention from other guests. At the end of the corridor, they looked back nonchalantly, then ducked into the stairwell. Becky pulled out a small radio from her purse.

"We have a hit," she whispered, and relayed the room number. The searchers had found the simulated nuclear device, which had been emitting a harmless amount of radiation, in less than two hours.

As if the searching weren't nerve-racking enough, operating the detectors requires great skill because the instruments, sensitive enough to home in on a bomb, can be confused by the soup of a metropolis' naturally occurring radiation. Freshly paved roads, yellow rest-room tiles, the Vermont granite used in some of Washington's federal buildings, a patient walking out of a hospital after radiation therapy, even a bunch of bananas can set off the detectors. Finding a nuclear bomb in a city, according to a searcher, "is like looking for a needle in a haystack of needles."

DISABLING BOMBS FROM MILES AWAY

NEST tries to neutralize a bomb without having its members come in physical contact with it. One way is to send out the Automated Tether-Operated Manipulator (ATOM), a wheeled robot with a remote-control arm. Via a long umbilical cord, ATOM can be managed from miles away. Stereo video cameras allow the teleoperator to see in front of the robot, while a third camera provides a closeup of the arm's gripping mechanism.

David Hughes, *Popular Mechanics*, January 1, 1996.

Though NEST has yet to find a nuclear device, the team has unearthed conventional bombs. The only case involving nuclear material involved an employee at a Wilmington, North Carolina, nuclear fuel plant who stole a small amount of low-grade uranium and threatened to disperse it. The FBI quickly recovered the uranium, and NEST didn't have to be summoned.

In case a real nuclear device ever is found, NEST's diagnostic and assessment teams have all kinds of equipment, such as portable X-ray machines, with which to peek under the bomb's wrapping. An instrument that looks like a Dustbuster is swept over the outside of the bomb to vacuum up any faint but telling fumes it might emit.

The disabling team has a number of ways to cripple a bomb. Working with Army demolition experts, they might decide to place their own bombs around the device and blow it up in such a way that the terrorist bomb's conventional explosives wouldn't set off its nuclear component (nuclear weapons always have both a conventional and a nuclear element). NEST also has a 30-mm cannon designed to blast a terrorist bomb into harmless pieces. Another option is to pour liquid nitrogen over the device to freeze its electronics.

If the bomb is a radiological dispersion device (that is, a conventional bomb larded with deadly radioactive shrapnel that will be scattered across a wide area) a special NEST team can quickly erect a nylon tent 35 ft. high and 50 ft. in diameter. Thirty thousand cubic feet of thick foam is then pumped into this "containment cone." When the terrorist's explosive is detonated, the tent is shredded, but the foam theoretically traps the radiological debris.

In various game-playing scenarios, NEST has imagined itself presenting the President of the U.S. with the worst choices of his life, choices he may have only minutes to make. In one apparently plausible scenario, there is a 10% chance that if NEST tries to defuse a bomb it will accidentally detonate with its full 10-kiloton yield, killing 100,000 Americans. But there's another choice: the bomb could be blown up in such a way that it would produce only a 1-kiloton yield, which would vaporize a mere 10,000 citizens. It will be cold comfort for survivors to know that the government has a special emergency room for just this eventuality at the Methodist Medical Center in Oak Ridge, Tennessee. Called the Radiation Emergency Assistance Center (REAC), it is the only E.R. in the country dedicated solely to treating nuclear-radiation patients.

Currently NEST doesn't operate overseas, where much of the nuclear danger lies. Russia and the other states with nuclear weapons still guard their atom bomb secrets closely. But scientists at the U.S. nuclear-weapons labs maintain back-channel contacts with their counterparts from the other nuclear countries, and Washington has begun selling Moscow special equipment for recovering and handling stolen weapons.

Some nuclear scientists like John Nuckolls, associate director at the DOE's Livermore lab, believe that America's nuclear preparedness team will eventually have to join others overseas in an international NEST force. "The destruction of any city in the world by nuclear terrorists would threaten all cities and nations," he insists. If so, we are all potential hostages. And the men and women of NEST may be the only ones who can come to the rescue.

PERIODICAL BIBLIOGRAPHY

The following articles have been selected to supplement the diverse views presented in this chapter. Addresses are provided for periodicals not indexed in the *Readers' Guide to Periodical Literature*, the *Alternative Press Index*, the *Social Sciences Index*, or the *Index to Legal Periodicals and Books*.

William J. Broad and Judith Miller	"Germ Defense Plan in Peril as Its Flaws Are Revealed," *New York Times*, August 7, 1998.
Seth Carus and Karl Lowe	"Chemical and Biological Terrorism: Threat and Response," *Policywatch*, May 12, 1997. Available from www.washingtoninstitute.org.
Stephen Chapman	"Surprise Missile Attacks and Other Delusions," *Conservative Chronicle*, July 29, 1998. Available from Box 37077, Boone, IA 50037-0077.
Richard L. Garwin	"Keeping Enemy Missiles at Bay," *New York Times*, July 28, 1998.
Lisbeth Gronlund and David Wright	"Missile Defense: The Sequel," *Technology Review*, May/June 1997.
William D. Hartung	"Spacey Missile Defense," *Nation*, July 27–August 3, 1998.
Fred C. Iklé	"Naked to Our Enemies," *Wall Street Journal*, March 10, 1997.
Melanie Kirkpatrick	"What's Blocking Missile Defense? A Defunct Treaty," *Wall Street Journal*, August 3, 1998.
Robert L. Shapiro et al.	"Botulism Surveillance and Emergency Response," *JAMA*, August 6, 1997. Available from the American Medical Association, PO Box 10946, Chicago, IL 60610-0946.

CHAPTER 4

WILL INTERNATIONAL TREATIES CURB WEAPONS PROLIFERATION?

CHAPTER PREFACE

During the Gulf War, Iraq admitted to having produced 260 liters of VX gas and 2,265 gallons of the anthrax bacteria—substances that are lethal in infinitesimal quantities. As a condition of the war's cease-fire, Iraq agreed to allow United Nations inspectors to destroy these weapons. However, because chemical and biological weapons facilities are easy to conceal—either by transporting the facilities themselves or by converting them to legitimate laboratories—Iraq has successfully kept its weapons hidden from UN inspectors.

Iraq's evasion of weapons inspectors has instigated debate over whether treaties or other agreements can adequately verify that countries are not producing or stockpiling chemical and biological weapons. Currently the possession of chemical and biological weapons is outlawed by two treaties: the Biological and Toxin Weapons Convention and the Chemical Weapons Convention. Experts disagree, however, about whether these treaties are effective in preventing weapons proliferation.

Proponents of weapons treaties maintain that more rigorous verification policies—such as random inspections of treaty members' biological and chemical research facilities—would help make the treaties enforceable. As former weapons inspector Jonathan B. Tucker notes, "The mere possibility of [inspections] could deter potential violators by making illicit production more risky and expensive." In addition, some analysts argue, treaties also prevent proliferation by establishing a moral and legal norm against certain weapons.

Others insist that chemical or biological weapons bans are always unenforceable. Scientist Alan P. Zelicoff contends that inspections are destined to fail: "Facilities engaged in legitimate activities can be incorrectly assessed to be in violation of the convention. Conversely, sites that are demonstrably in compliance . . . easily can convert to illicit activities within hours after the departure of inspectors." Treaty critics maintain that the only thing weapons treaties accomplish is to disarm peaceful countries—while hostile nations remain free to amass more weapons.

The controversy over weapons treaties reflects the question of whether laws can effectively deter the production and use of weapons of mass destruction. In the chapter that follows, security experts, policy makers, and others debate the benefits and disadvantages of four treaties that are intended to prevent weapons proliferation: the Chemical Weapons Convention, the Comprehensive Nuclear Test Ban Treaty, the Biological and Toxin Weapons Convention, and the Nuclear Non-Proliferation Treaty.

"The safety of our troops and the security of our nation will be strengthened by the [chemical weapons convention]."

CHEMICAL WEAPONS SHOULD BE BANNED

William S. Cohen

In the following viewpoint, William S. Cohen, the secretary of defense, argues in favor of the Chemical Weapons Convention (CWC), an international treaty banning the production and use of chemical weapons. Cohen contends that the CWC will prevent the proliferation of these weapons, thereby reducing the risk of chemical warfare.

As you read, consider the following questions:
1. According to Cohen, why is the CWC verifiable?
2. In the author's opinion, what effect will the CWC have on U.S. industry?
3. How should the United States deter regional aggressors, in Cohen's view?

Abridged from William S. Cohen, "Ratify the Chemical Weapons Treaty," *The Washington Post National Weekly Edition*, April 14, 1997. Reprinted with permission of the author.

In ancient times, Greek city-states assailed enemies with the noxious fumes of smoldering pitch and sulfur while Chinese warriors wafted arsenic-laced smoke screens against their foes. As we approach the next millennium, we face the prospect of regional aggressors, third-rate armies, terrorist cells and even religious cults unleashing lethal chemical agents against our troops in the field and our people at home.

A paradox of the new strategic environment is that American military superiority actually increases the threat of chemical attacks against us by creating incentives for adversaries to challenge us not directly but asymmetrically through nonconventional means.

A National Response to Chemical Weapons

Dealing with this threat requires a coherent national response involving: active and passive defenses; continued efforts to limit the spread of chemical weapons technology; improved intelligence collection and threat analysis; well-coordinated civil defense capabilities; and an international standard barring the production and possession of chemical weapons. Central to this response is the Chemical Weapons Convention (CWC).

President Ronald Reagan decided that the United States should stop producing chemical weapons and begin destroying our arsenal. The CWC, negotiated under Presidents Reagan and George Bush, would require other countries to do the same. . . .

Myths About the CWC

Critics of the CWC have made several assertions that must be considered—and rejected.

• *Verification:* The CWC includes the most intense verification regime ever negotiated. Some bemoan imperfections in the CWC's verification arrangements and the prospect that some countries will seek to cheat. Verification is never perfect. What matters is that large-scale violations be detectable, and the CWC meets this test. Moreover, the CWC's comprehensive and intrusive verification regime will improve our ability to monitor possible chemical weapons proliferation—which we must do with or without the CWC.

• *Rogue States:* It's argued that only law-abiding nations will respect it, not those we trust least. Most industrialized nations have agreed to destroy their chemical stocks and forswear further development or production, so the CWC will reduce the chemical weapons problem to a few notorious rogues and impose trade restrictions that will curb their ability to obtain the materials to make chemical agents.

If the CWC fails, we should expect chemical weapons to proliferate to even more countries than now possess them, raising the risk they could be used against U.S. troops not only by regional aggressors but even in peacekeeping and other situations.

MINIMIZING THE THREAT OF CHEMICAL WEAPONS

Chemical weapons are inherently genocidal. They have little effect on well-equipped military forces but they kill unprotected civilians. Chemical weapons have not been part of U.S. military strategy for years.

Indeed, the United States is already destroying its stocks of chemical weapons; the treaty [banning chemical weapons] requires the rest of the world to do what the United States is already doing.

The key strategic task facing the United States is to minimize the threat of weapons of mass destruction in the hands of adversary states or terrorists. In an anarchic world, chemical weapons threaten people in even the strongest nations. . . .

Some treaty opponents argue that the treaty will lull our political leaders into relaxing our chemical weapons defenses. Instead, they say, the United States should retain chemical weapons and announce that if anyone dares to trifle with the United States, it does so at its peril. Deterrence is all.

That makes little sense. The United States has conventional weapons that are far more capable than chemical weapons of an effective retaliatory response.

The CWC does not offer ironclad security guarantees; no reasonable person should expect that of any treaty. But the treaty would add law enforcement to the U.S. arsenal.

Military leaders and politicians in both parties have repeatedly affirmed that the CWC would reduce the risk that adversaries of the United States would acquire chemical weapons, and it would make it more likely that clandestine efforts would be detected.

Barry Kellman and Edward A. Tanzman, *Bulletin of the Atomic Scientists*, January/ February 1997.

• *Technology Transfer:* Critics assert the CWC obligates member states to exchange manufacturing technology that can be used to make chemical agents. In fact, nothing in the CWC requires any weakening of our export controls, and the United States would continue to work in the "Australia Group" to maintain and make more effective internationally agreed controls on chemical and biological weapons technology. [The Australia Group is an informal group of countries that are committed to combatting the proliferation of chemical and biological weapons.] Indeed, the CWC establishes strict trade restrictions on precursor chemicals, prohibiting state parties from helping others to acquire a chemical weapons capability.

• *U.S. Industry:* American chemical companies that will be most affected by the CWC strongly support it and view its requirements as reasonable and manageable—which is not surprising, since they played a key advisory role during the CWC's negotiations. And small businesses initially troubled by critics' claims that the CWC would be a costly regulatory nightmare now agree that the alarms are false. . . .

• *Chemical Defense:* Opponents suggest that ratification of the CWC will reduce our support for defensive measures. In fact, the opposite is true: The Department of Defense not only maintains a robust program to equip and train the troops against chemical and biological attack, we have asked Congress to increase this program's budget by almost $225 million. In addition, we will proceed with our theater missile defense programs and robust intelligence efforts against the chemical threat.

• *Counter Threats:* In the 1980s, I led the congressional fight to build binary chemical weapons to deter Soviet chemical use in Europe. With the end of the Cold War, the world has changed. Regional aggressors can be deterred by our vow to respond with overwhelming and devastating force to a chemical attack. Our military commanders agree that threatening chemical retaliation is not necessary, and they support the CWC—as do retired military leaders such as Colin Powell and Norman Schwarzkopf.

The safety of our troops and the security of our nation will be strengthened by the CWC.

| "Banning chemical weapons . . . is not merely inadvisable but downright dangerous."

BANNING CHEMICAL WEAPONS IS DANGEROUS

Thomas Sowell

Thomas Sowell, a nationally syndicated columnist, contends in the following viewpoint that the Chemical Weapons Convention cannot fulfill its promise of banning chemical weapons. According to Sowell, an international ban against chemical weapons will not prevent aggressor nations from developing or using chemical weapons.

As you read, consider the following questions:
1. According to Sowell, why didn't Hitler employ his chemical weapons against the Allies?
2. What is the "joke" of disarmament treaties, according to the author?
3. Why would violations of the chemical weapons treaty be difficult to detect, in the author's opinion?

Abridged from Thomas Sowell, "Dismal Record of Treaties," *The Washington Times*, April 24, 1997. Reprinted by permission of Thomas Sowell and Creators Syndicate. All rights reserved.

The treaty to ban chemical weapons is another painful reminder of how easily we are misled by words. Who could possibly be against banning chemical weapons? The real question is whether this treaty—or any treaty—can actually do that.

Many people with military backgrounds, including past Defense Secretaries Caspar Weinberger and James Schlesinger, oppose the treaty precisely because it will increase the dangers, rather than reduce them. Politicians from both parties have lined up on the opposite side, in favor of the treaty, because it makes more sense politically than it does militarily. . . .

But, when it comes to what the treaty is supposedly about—banning chemical weapons—it is not merely inadvisable but downright dangerous.

Ask yourself: Why did Adolf Hitler not use chemical weapons against the Allies during World War II, especially since he had no qualms about chemically killing millions of defenseless civilians in his concentration camps? The answer is that he knew gassing Americans would lead to Americans gassing far more Germans.

We had chemical weapons, and he knew it. That is why Hitler didn't use his. There is nothing complicated about this—either then or now. What gets complicated is trying to evade the obvious, in the interest of scoring political points by being on the side of the angels and denouncing chemical weapons.

All weapons are harmful. That is what makes them weapons. It is shortsighted grandstanding for politicians to pretend to be banning weapons that they cannot in fact ban. But that is what makes them politicians.

The joke in all sorts of disarmament treaties throughout the twentieth century has been that peaceful nations tend to abide by them while aggressors violate them. That is how Britain got suckered in its naval treaty with Nazi Germany in the 1930s and how both Britain and the United States got suckered in their naval treaty with Japan before that.

Men paid with their lives during World War II for these prewar political charades that allowed aggressor nations to gain military advantages while peaceful nations held back from building the military deterrents that were needed. For the first two years of that war, the democracies did not win a single major battle against the totalitarian powers—and not many minor battles either.

Eventually, the tide turned, after the United States belatedly began to build up its military forces, but it was touch and go for quite a while. In an age of devastating chemical and nuclear warfare, there may not be any second chances.

Reprinted by permission of Chuck Asay and Creators Syndicate.

Some of the most dangerous countries in the world today are not even going to sign the so-called chemical weapons ban treaty. This is an invitation for us to disarm ourselves of a chemical weapons deterrent, while people like Saddam Hussein remain free to use theirs.

As for other major powers that plan to sign the treaty, how are we to verify whether they will live up to it? And even if we discover that China, for example, is not living up to the treaty, what can we do about it then? Start a war?

Even small powers can build up devastating chemical arsenals because they require no huge facilities. That is also why violations of the treaty can be very difficult to detect, until it is too late.

Why is something so militarily dangerous so politically popular? Mushy wishful thinking on the part of too many Americans, and a cynical exploitation of their feelings by politicians.

Every ban on any kind of weapon—nuclear, chemical or other—is sure to be greeted by cheers in the media. The specifics of these treaties receive little attention. Apparently it's the thought that counts.

Actually, it is the feelings that count politically, since very little thought goes into many of these feelings. Both at home and abroad, those who want weapons banned on paper seldom pause to think that peaceful people are much easier to disarm than violent people—and disarming peaceful people just shifts the balance of power in favor of aggressors, increasing the very dangers you are trying to reduce.

"[A nuclear testing ban] eases the fear that some country will achieve a technological coup and surprise its neighbors with a new form of diabolical weapon."

A NUCLEAR TEST BAN WILL PREVENT NUCLEAR PROLIFERATION

C. Dale White

The Comprehensive Nuclear Test Ban Treaty, signed by President Bill Clinton in September 1996 and currently awaiting ratification by the Senate, forbids test explosions of nuclear weapons. In the following viewpoint, C. Dale White maintains that the test ban treaty would establish a global norm against nuclear testing, strengthen U.S. and international security, and prevent the proliferation of nuclear weapons. A retired bishop, White speaks and writes about issues related to global peace.

As you read, consider the following questions:
1. Why is the test ban treaty "an historic achievement," in the author's view?
2. According to White, how does the world's reaction to France's nuclear tests illustrate the power of global norms?
3. How does White counter the argument that a nuclear test ban cannot be verified?

Excerpted from C. Dale White, "Toward a Global Norm: No More Nuclear Testing," *Christian Social Action*, March 1998. Reprinted with permission from *Christian Social Action* magazine; © General Board of Church and Society of the United Methodist Church.

After 40 years of bipartisan effort, in September 1996 President Bill Clinton was the first global leader to sign the Comprehensive Nuclear Test Ban Treaty (CTBT). He has now sent it to the Senate for ratification. The U.S. military, 70 percent of the American people, and more than 140 nations, including the major nuclear powers, support the treaty. . . .

What does the treaty require? While it is 92 pages long, the heart of the treaty is the first sentence of Article I:

"Each state party undertakes not to carry out any nuclear weapon test explosion, or any other nuclear explosion, and to prohibit and prevent any such nuclear explosion at any place under its jurisdiction or control."

This puts to an end a period of more than four decades during which the world witnessed the explosion of at least 2,000 nuclear explosions in the air, underground, and underwater. Finally we dare to hope that "the downwinders," guinea pigs for "national security" dogma, will rest easier. They may take heart that others will not have to suffer as they have suffered. . . .

The treaty has some serious limitations. India has refused to sign out of concern that the treaty does not ban tests through laboratory experiments, computer simulations and "zero yield" underground tests. [Zero yield nuclear tests are detonations that have no explosive power.] . . .

Another serious limitation is that the treaty will not enter into force until all 44 countries, including India, that possess nuclear weapons or nuclear power reactors ratify it. India has announced that it will never be pressured to sign it as long as the nuclear nations make no commitment to destroy their weapons by a specified time.

AN HISTORIC ACHIEVEMENT

With all of these limitations, the Test Ban Treaty remains an historic achievement. It eases the fear that some country will achieve a technological coup and surprise its neighbors with a new form of diabolical weapon. Such an event would be terribly dangerous. It would be destabilizing as it altered the balance of power in the world. It would usher in a new nuclear arms race. Even the most dedicated militarist could hardly wish for that!

Some will argue that since India has announced it will never sign, the treaty will never become international law. It will gather dust in the archives. We will hear some of the same arguments opponents used against the Chemical Weapons Treaty. . . .

Verification will be impossible, they will say. They will argue that Russia routinely ignores its international agreements, while the United States keeps its word. Rogue nations will gain dangerous new power as responsible nations disarm. Our national security and sovereignty will be compromised. In addition, some will argue that the safety and dependability of our current weapons cannot be assured without nuclear explosions.

In the face of such attacks, why should we work to see that the treaty is ratified?

• *The treaty establishes a global moral standard* that over 140 nations including the major nuclear nations have agreed to honor. In the words of Ambassador Richard Butler of Australia, who introduced the treaty to the UN General Assembly:

> "It will stand first of all as the unique expression by the world community of a norm—a political, moral, and hopefully ultimately a firmly enshrined legal norm—that no one should ever conduct a nuclear test explosion. As every day passes and that norm is observed, then it becomes harder and harder politically in international relations, and even in domestic politics, for a government to make the decision to break that norm."

THE COMPREHENSIVE TEST BAN TREATY
WILL CURB NUCLEAR PROLIFERATION

The Comprehensive Test Ban Treaty (CTBT) marks an historic milestone in efforts to reduce the nuclear threat and build a safer world. The CTBT will prohibit any nuclear explosion whether for weapons or peaceful purposes. The cessation of all nuclear weapon test explosions and all other nuclear explosions, by constraining the development and qualitative improvement of nuclear weapons, constitutes an effective measure of nuclear disarmament and nonproliferation in all its aspects. It will thus contribute effectively to the prevention of nuclear proliferation and the process of nuclear disarmament and enhance international peace and security.

U.S. Newswire, *White House Fact Sheet on Purpose of Comprehensive Test Ban Treaty*, September 23, 1997.

Those who doubt the power of such a global moral commitment should remember France's experience. Ignoring world public opinion, it cynically resumed nuclear testing in the Pacific immediately after signing the extension of the Nuclear Non-Proliferation Treaty. To win the votes of the non-nuclear nations, the nuclear nations had solemnly assured them that they would work to end all testing. Now France was testing again.

The people of the world rose up in protest. Spontaneous boycotts of French products in international markets soon hurt the

French people in a sensitive spot—their pocketbooks! France hastened to conclude its testing and announced that it would close down its testing site on the Mururoa Atoll in the Pacific.

• *Ratification of the treaty will strengthen U.S. security, and the security of the entire world.*

The critical issue of *verification* will be hotly debated in the Senate. Can we be sure that other nations will not cheat on their obligations? The answer is that a vast network of monitoring systems will be put in place under the treaty. A global array of seismic, radionuclide, hydroacoustic and infrasound monitoring stations will be deployed. Nuclear explosions with any military significance will be detected.

In addition, for the first time all nuclear-capable nations will agree to on-site inspections if the monitoring systems detect a suspicious event. In January 1998 a seismic event occurred in Russia that some charge could have been a clandestine nuclear explosion. Others say it was only an earthquake. Under the new treaty, teams of experts could travel to the site for a closer look.

HALTING NUCLEAR PROLIFERATION

The *non-proliferation* issue will enter into Senate debate. Will the treaty help to halt the spread of nuclear weapons to other nations? Many strategists believe that nuclear proliferation will be the greatest threat to the peace in the future. As President Clinton said in his UN address in 1996, the nations of the world must unite against "21st century predators." He warned, "We're vulnerable to the reckless act of rogue states and an unholy axis of terrorists, drug traffickers and international criminals."

No treaty can totally guarantee that a renegade nation or terrorist group would be prevented from creating a crude nuclear device. Yet the deployment of a modern nuclear arsenal would be virtually impossible once the monitoring and intelligence systems are in place under the new treaty.

"[The nuclear test ban] will probably have the opposite of its desired effect and actually increase the danger arising to the United States from the proliferation of nuclear arms."

A NUCLEAR TEST BAN WILL NOT PREVENT NUCLEAR PROLIFERATION

The Center for Security Policy

The Comprehensive Nuclear Test Ban Treaty proposes to make nuclear testing illegal under international law. In the following viewpoint, the Center for Security Policy contends that the test ban is unenforceable and will do nothing to deter nuclear proliferation. Furthermore, the organization asserts, the United States depends on nuclear testing to maintain the safety and effectiveness of its nuclear arsenal. The Center for Security Policy is a nonprofit, nonpartisan organization that examines and comments on all aspects of security policy, especially issues relating to the foreign, defense, economic, and technological interests of the United States.

As you read, consider the following questions:

1. What example does the author provide of the nuclear test ban's unverifiability?
2. What will prevent the nuclear test ban from being enacted globally, according to the Center for Security Policy?
3. In the organization's view, why will the nuclear test ban be an ineffective impediment to nuclear proliferation?

Excerpted from the Center for Security Policy, "Clinton's C.T.B. and Other Placebos Won't Stop, Will Compound the Danger of Proliferating Weapons of Mass Destruction," *Decision Brief*, Publications of the Center for Security Policy, no. 96-D 90, September 24, 1996. Endnotes in the original have been omitted in this reprint. Reprinted with permission.

President Bill Clinton chose the United Nations (UN) as the backdrop for consummating one of the most cherished foreign policy goals of the "denuclearizers" that dominate his Administration—the Comprehensive Test Ban Treaty (CTB). He called it "the longest-sought, hardest fought prize in arms control history." As has so often been true in the checkered history of arms control, however, this "prize" is much less than is being claimed for it.

For example, on September 10, 1996, the director of the Clinton Administration's Arms Control and Disarmament Agency, John Hollum, asserted that the UN General Assembly's approval of the CTB—an action several critical steps removed from its global entry into force—meant that "the nuclear danger has just been reduced." This statement is approximately as misleading and irresponsible as President Clinton's oft-repeated declaration that "not a single Russian missile is pointed at the children of America."

Indeed, like so many well-intentioned but ultimately defective arms control accords before it, the CTB will probably have the opposite of its desired effect and actually *increase* the danger arising to the United States from the proliferation of nuclear arms.

ANOTHER UNVERIFIABLE TREATY

Violations of the Clinton Comprehensive Test Ban cannot be detected or proven with high confidence. What was already a difficult task has been made more so by concessions regarding on-site inspections in the negotiating end-game demanded by China as its price for signing the CTB. Notably, it will take the approval of 30 countries out of the 51-member multilateral "Executive Committee" before an on-site challenge inspection can be conducted. As a practical matter, it is difficult to get thirty countries to agree what day of the week it is. It will be exceedingly problematic to get them to agree to an intrusive inspection over the objections of nations like Russia or China.

The CTB's unverifiability is not an academic issue. In January 1996, the Department of Defense received indications consistent with an underground nuclear test in Russia—even though Moscow claims that it has been observing a self-imposed moratorium on nuclear testing. And the former Defense Nuclear Agency (now called the Defense Special Weapons Agency) has reported that there are several techniques that could be employed to reduce the likelihood that covert nuclear tests will be reliably identified *even by in-country seismic monitoring*.

What is more, even if the CTB had effective on-site inspection provisions, past experience suggests that the U.S. government would be reluctant to employ them in a manner that would prove other state parties—especially preeminent ones like Russia and China—were in violation. This is an especially unlikely prospect given the enormous political capital expended by the Clinton Administration in securing this accord in the first place.

A CTB WILL NOT BE GLOBAL

The government of India has vowed never to sign the CTB. As drafted, that refusal by a nuclear weapons-capable state will mean that the treaty will not come into force. India—and perhaps other states that choose to follow New Delhi's example—will be able legally to continue to conduct nuclear tests.

Gary Brookins/*Richmond Times-Dispatch*. Reprinted with permission.

Unless the Senate rejects the CTB, however, the United States would be obliged by international legal practice to take no action that would violate or undercut the treaty's terms. As a result, the U.S. could find itself permanently enjoined from testing even though others continue to engage in it, legally or illegally.

A CTB WILL NOT BE AN EFFECTIVE
IMPEDIMENT TO NUCLEAR PROLIFERATION

The CTB simply will not prevent—just as the Nuclear Non-Proliferation Treaty has not prevented—non-nuclear states who want nuclear weapons from acquiring them, frequent claims by proponents to the contrary notwithstanding. This is because it is no longer necessary for nuclear wannabe states to develop their own weapons; today, they can simply buy fully validated components or, for that matter, complete and previously tested nuclear devices on the international arms market.

It is also the case that, if one is willing to settle for a relatively crude atomic weapon—to say nothing of radiological weapons (i.e., weapons that use conventional explosives rather than fission to scatter lethal radioactive materials)—such devices can be developed without conducting underground nuclear tests. For example, the U.S. atomic bomb dropped on Nagasaki in 1945 was of a design that had not been subjected to an explosive test beforehand.

WHY A CTB WILL COMPOUND THE DANGER OF NUCLEAR PROLIFERATION

If a CTB will not stop other nations from developing or otherwise acquiring nuclear weapons, it will almost certainly impair the U.S. ability to deal with the resulting threat through its own nuclear deterrent capabilities. This result can be predicted since the highly sophisticated weapons that comprise the current U.S. nuclear stockpile were created on the assumption that actual weapons testing would continue to be available. Accordingly, in order for the United States to maintain an effective, safe and reliable—and therefore credible—nuclear deterrent, it is necessary to perform periodic detonations of actual weapons. Successive U.S. presidents, including Jimmy Carter, have declined to complete a comprehensive ban on nuclear testing for this reason, among others.

The reliability of America's nuclear arsenal will also be degraded by a further immutable fact of life: It takes highly skilled, experienced and dedicated professionals to sustain the U.S. nuclear deterrent force. Since the United States began a unilateral, uninspected moratorium on nuclear testing, it has lost the services of many of the best and most knowledgeable technicians skilled in using periodic testing to assure the nuclear stockpile worked when it was supposed to—and does not when it is not supposed to. That loss cannot be fully offset by the computer modeling technology. . . .

The greatest cost of all arising from the Clinton Administration's naive effort to use arms control agreements to deal with the threat of proliferating weapons of mass destruction may be the false sense of security induced by these unverifiable and ineffectual agreements. That illusion is sure to be shattered—possibly at great loss of life and national treasure—in the future.

> "As long as governments and would-be terrorists think they can get what they want by waving a bit of anthrax around, we desperately need a [biological weapons] treaty."

THE BIOLOGICAL WEAPONS BAN MUST BE STRENGTHENED

Debora MacKenzie

The Biological Weapons Convention (BWC), which bans the possession of biological weapons, went into effect in 1972 after being ratified by 140 countries. Debora MacKenzie asserts in the following viewpoint that the BWC should be strengthened to include enforcement measures. According to the author, one such measure—random inspections of biological facilities—would help detect treaty violators. MacKenzie is the Brussels correspondent for *New Scientist*, a weekly science magazine.

As you read, consider the following questions:

1. According to MacKenzie, what lessons about biological weapons inspections have been learned from recent experiences with Iraq?
2. Why is the U.S. position on biological weapons inspections flawed, in the author's opinion?
3. What reason does President Bill Clinton provide for rejecting random inspections of biological facilities, as cited by the author?

Reprinted from Debora MacKenzie, "Put Teeth into the Germ Warfare Treaty," *Newsday*, April 20, 1998, by permission of the *New Scientist*, London.

The United States and its allies go to the brink of war to get United Nations (UN) inspectors into guarded buildings where Iraq may be hiding biological weapons. And a Russian defector to the United States, once a high-ranking official in the Soviet germ warfare program, says Russia continues to develop biological weapons under the guise of defensive research.

One thing has become clear: Whatever the UN team finds in Saddam Hussein's palaces, the world will be only marginally safer from the threat of germ warfare as a result of the inspection. That's because there is little to stop another nation or another fanatic or even Iraq, once the inspectors go home, from going after the perverse power that a bit of anthrax or botulin toxin has given Hussein. There is only one real answer: Watch everyone by finally giving some teeth to the 1972 Biological Weapons Convention.

The 140 countries that belong to the convention, including the United States, Iraq and Russia, have renounced using germs and their toxins as weapons. But there are no legal means to check whether members are keeping their promises. Even Iraq could not be inspected for biological weapons without special permission from the UN Security Council.

In March 1998 in Geneva, treaty members tried again to put verification procedures into the agreement. The talks have been hamstrung by President Bill Clinton's refusal to consider a type of inspection that European Union countries, and most others, think is essential to deter prospective biowarriors.

LEARNING FROM IRAQ

While there are big differences between the United Nations' unfriendly inspections in Iraq and the friendly, just-checking sorts of inspections proposed for the treaty, the Iraqi experience has taught us what works. Technical experts must be free to go anywhere—breweries, biotech companies, fertilizer plants that are perfectly legitimate but easily converted to disease factories—at random, on short notice. There are two major objectors to this approach: Russia and the United States.

Russia was one of the major backers of the 1972 treaty. Yet in 1992, it admitted that it had kept its own bioweapons program running all along. Indeed, it may still exist. Russia also rejects every kind of inspection but the kind forced on Iraq.

WHY RANDOM INSPECTIONS ARE NEEDED

Russia wields little moral force in the negotiations. The U.S. position, however, is crucial to an agreement. But Clinton wants inspections under the treaty only when there is already obvious cause for suspicion, say, an odd disease outbreak. Such clumsiness is rare, and when it occurs things have already gone too far.

Russia suffered one such incident back in 1979 with an outbreak of anthrax downwind of its closed military facilities in Sverdlovsk, now called Yekaterinburg. In 1998, the world learned, from Russian defector Kanatjan Alibekov, just how immense Russia's germ warfare program was, and possibly still is, yet the anthrax incident was the only time the outside world had an obvious cause for suspicion.

A Need for Tough Enforcement Measures

The Biological Weapons Convention has been in force since 1972, but frankly, it lacks the teeth of tough enforcement measures. We must strengthen that treaty with an international inspection system to help detect and deter cheating.

The White House, *Fact Sheet: The Biological Weapons Convention*, January 27, 1998.

And what about prospective biowarriors messing with diseases more common than anthrax—severe food poisoning, for instance; would an escape of those germs raise anyone's suspicions? Even Iraq would not have attracted a suspicion-based inspection in the 1980s, when its bioweapons program might have been nipped in the bud.

Clinton argues on behalf of the U.S. pharmaceuticals and biotech industries that random inspections are unacceptable because they will expose trade secrets. But there are straightforward technical means of allowing inspectors to look for incriminating evidence without revealing a confidential gene sequence or production process.

Some negotiators in Geneva are privately questioning whether the United States isn't hiding behind the worries of its biotech companies to avoid inspections that might reveal more biological weapons research than Washington would like to admit.

A highly speculative, and in any case avoidable, threat to industrial profit should not be allowed to undermine the creation of an inspection regime that might actually prevent the next Saddam. As long as governments and would-be terrorists think they can get what they want by waving a bit of anthrax around, we desperately need a treaty with all the teeth it can get.

"There is no way to make the
[biological weapons ban] verifiable
or enforceable."

THE BIOLOGICAL WEAPONS BAN IS
INHERENTLY INEFFECTIVE

Frank J. Gaffney Jr.

Frank J. Gaffney Jr. maintains in the following viewpoint that because biological weapons can easily be manufactured in secret, international bans against biological weapons will always be ineffective. Instead of wasting efforts on unenforceable treaties, Gaffney contends, the United States should focus on policies that will deter biological warfare, such as export controls and defenses against ballistic missiles. Gaffney is the director for the Center for Security Policy, a nonprofit, nonpartisan organization that studies and reports on all aspects of security policy. He is also a columnist for the *Washington Times*.

As you read, consider the following questions:
1. Why is it easy for nations or terrorist groups to manufacture biological weapons in secret, as cited by the author?
2. In Gaffney's view, what will be the economic impact of modifying the Biological Weapons Convention?
3. According to the author, what steps should the U.S. take to reduce the risk of biological warfare?

Abridged from Frank J. Gaffney Jr., "Sounds of a Biological Ticking Clock," *The Washington Times*, February 24, 1998. Reprinted by permission of *The Washington Times*.

The February 1998 news flash from Las Vegas should be a wake-up call for the American people. The fact that two men were arrested by the FBI and charged with "pos[ing] a chemical and biological threat to our community" literally brings home the implications of the danger posed by Saddam Hussein: The burgeoning threat of biological warfare (BW) can no longer be ignored or regarded as a problem only for those unlucky enough to live in or near Iraq.

This is true even though the Las Vegas episode, like the BW scare at the Washington headquarters of the B'nai Brith in the spring of 1997, fortuitously appear to have involved false alarms. The unhappy reality is that Saddam Hussein is not the only bad guy with large quantities of deadly viruses at his disposal. In fact, virtually all of this country's potential adversaries are believed to have biological weapons in their arsenals. And even without the help of state-sponsors, the technology to cultivate and disseminate diseases like anthrax and botulism are readily available to determined terrorists.

ADDRESSING THE THREAT OF BIOLOGICAL WARFARE

This terrifying state of affairs makes several conclusions inescapable, including the following:

• Arms control can't address the danger of biological warfare: The Clinton administration's reflexive response to the hemorrhage of biological weapons capabilities—and indeed, most other forms of weapons of mass destruction (WMD) proliferation—has been to seek arms control "solutions" to the problem. Despite the abject failure in Iraq of the most comprehensive monitoring scheme ever undertaken to find, limit and destroy such weapons, President Bill Clinton announced in his 1998 State of the Union address that he would dispatch a team to negotiate amendments to the 1972 Biological Weapons Convention (BWC) intended to "strengthen the enforcement provisions of the BWC."

The unalterable facts of life are that there is no way to make the BWC verifiable or enforceable. As Alan Zelicoff, a scientist at Sandia National Laboratory who has participated in the U.S. government's interagency deliberations on "enhancing" the BWC, recently wrote in the *Washington Post:*

> Equipment for pharmaceutical production is identical to that used for bio-weapons processing, and even the most toxic of biological materials are used in medical therapeutics and research. [Furthermore,] in just a few days or weeks, biological weapons can be manufactured in militarily significant quantities in a site no larger than a small house.

While reworking the BWC will not improve that treaty, it will add enormously to its costs. The initiatives the president unveiled in his State of the Union speech would have a particularly devastating effect on some of the nation's most dynamic and productive companies—the American biotech and pharmaceutical industries. Some of these companies could literally be destroyed by the loss of billions of dollars' worth of proprietary information compromised in the course of an arms control inspection. Alternatively, they might be irreparably harmed by the besmirching of a business reputation should competitors use the treaty process groundlessly to charge that a U.S. concern is now, or has been, engaged in biological warfare programs.

THE BWC CANNOT BE ENFORCED

Biological weapons can be made with readily available commercial technology in small facilities, such as wineries or hospital or pharmaceutical labs. Even if a regime of stringent inspections is set up to attempt to detect cheating on the Biological Weapons Convention (BWC), it will fail to stop the spread of such weapons. The stringent monitoring of Iraq's biological weapons program has been unable to guarantee that all of its biological material was destroyed. And even in the unlikely event that all of the material were destroyed, Iraq or any other country that wanted to cheat could produce more of it at any one of numerous commercial facilities. In short, the BWC is unenforceable.

Ivan Eland, CATO Commentary, July 13, 1998.

• There is an urgent need for new, effective export controls: Instead of pursuing arms control will-of-the-wisps in response to the BW threat, the Clinton administration should be strengthening mechanisms whereby rogue states and potential suppliers alike can be convinced that there will be real costs imposed upon those who engage in the unauthorized and reckless transfer of relevant [weapons] technology. Unfortunately, the administration has engaged in a wrecking operation on the unilateral and multilateral export control regime it inherited.

• The present U.S. posture of "assured vulnerability" must be corrected at once: The most troublesome aspect of the threat posed by biological and chemical weapons is that the United States lacks any defenses, passive or active, against these weapons. Incredibly, President Clinton and to an even greater extent Vice President Al Gore are opposed to active defenses (that is, weapons that counter attacking weapons) for the American homeland.

They have also eschewed to date measures that would provide appreciable passive defenses (for example, civil defense measures) for the American people.

The reason: Such programs run counter to the theology of "assured vulnerability" codified in the 1972 Anti-Ballistic Missile Treaty. Unbeknownst to most Americans, this accord effectively prohibits the United States from having competent missile defenses. In practice, though, the Clinton administration has rationalized the assured vulnerability to missile attack dictated by this so-called "cornerstone of strategic stability" as an excuse for leaving the United States exposed to all other forms of homeland defense.

MITIGATING U.S. VULNERABILITY

Mitigation of this posture of vulnerability must be an urgent priority for the United States. For starters, the nation must urgently field effective, global defenses against missile attack (both ballistic and cruise missiles). The United States must also provide passive defenses for its people that are at least as capable of responding to an imminent threat as have been Israel's gas-mask distribution and civil defense services.

It is ironic that President Clinton has declared in successive Executive Orders that proliferation of weapons of mass destruction is "an unusual and extraordinary threat to the national security, foreign policy and economy of the United States." The Las Vegas wake-up call reminds us there is not a moment to lose in making this quintessential bit of empty Clinton rhetoric into a genuine catalyst for urgent changes in U.S. policy and programs needed to address what truly is an "unusual and extraordinary threat."

"Without the [Nuclear Non-
Proliferation Treaty] we would have
seen new nuclear states emerge in
troubled regions around the globe."

THE NUCLEAR NON-PROLIFERATION TREATY FURTHERS NUCLEAR DISARMAMENT

Madeleine K. Albright

Under the Nuclear Non-Proliferation Treaty (NPT), which took effect in 1970, 181 non-nuclear countries have agreed not to develop nuclear capabilities, while the five declared nuclear powers—the U.S., Britain, France, China, and Russia—have pledged to work toward nuclear disarmament. Madeleine K. Albright, the current Secretary of State and former U.S. Ambassador to the United Nations, argues in the following viewpoint that the NPT has curbed the spread of nuclear weapons by making nuclear proliferation punishable by international law.

As you read, consider the following questions:

1. In Albright's view, what arms control accomplishments have been made possible by the NPT?
2. How will the indefinite extension of the NPT prevent nuclear proliferation, according to Albright?
3. How is the NPT enforced, in the author's words?

Reprinted from Madeleine K. Albright, "Breaking Up the Nuclear Family," *New Perspectives Quarterly*, Summer 1995, by permission of Blackwell Publishers, copyright 1995.

After a long diplomatic campaign, led by President Bill Clinton and Vice President Al Gore, the nations of the world agreed in 1995 to make permanent the quarter-century-old and about-to-expire Nuclear Non-Proliferation Treaty—the NPT. In a world that sometimes seems ever more dangerous and uncertain, this decision is a milestone.

By making the NPT permanent, we have helped advance what is perhaps America's highest priority in foreign policy—preventing the spread of nuclear weapons into the hands of a hostile power or terrorists.

The NPT has not had a perfect record. But it has turned the development of a nuclear bomb from a celebration of nationalist pride and power, as it was threatening to become in the 1960s, into a violation of international law subject to inspections and condemnation. The treaty has prompted a number of countries that once planned to develop nuclear capabilities to give up that ambition. It has caused others to slow or freeze nuclear programs. It has deterred many others from starting down that road. Without the NPT, we would have seen new nuclear states emerge in troubled regions around the globe.

As a result of diplomatic determination, the treaty was extended forever. By avoiding a 10- or 20-year deadline, countries need not develop a nuclear program to hedge against the day that the ban would expire. Now, nearly all countries of the world have committed themselves never to obtain nuclear weapons. Meanwhile, the five "declared" nuclear powers (the U.S., Britain, France, China and Russia) have pledged to redouble our already-productive efforts to reduce nuclear stockpiles and nuclear testing, and to ensure that nuclear technology is made available to those who will use it only for peaceful purposes, such as energy and medical research.

To Americans, this diplomatic achievement shows the value of acting with others through the UN system. Like it or not, stopping nuclear proliferation requires the active support of other countries and international institutions. Indeed, we used every diplomatic tool and every international forum to convince individual countries of the benefits to them of a permanent treaty. America, or other nations, simply can't "go it alone" when it comes to key objectives like non-proliferation.

Of course, extending the treaty is only a first step. It will be up to the International Atomic Energy Agency (IAEA) to ensure that countries that have signed the NPT meet their commitments not to develop nuclear weapons. Whenever countries receive nuclear technology, this specialized agency of the UN inspects facilities and monitors operations to see that the material is being used only for the purposes allowed.

The system is by no means foolproof, since countries can keep inspectors away from sites that would expose their duplicity. That is why the U.S. will continue to rely on its own intelligence resources to alert us to nuclear dangers. Nevertheless, having a credible policing agency gives us a window on nuclear programs we would not otherwise have. Only the IAEA has the mandate to oversee the nuclear programs of countries like Iraq and North Korea, and to report violations that require international action.

THE ROLE OF THE NPT

Since it took effect in 1970, the NPT has been the most important means of easing nuclear anxieties around the world. It provides countries with reasonable assurances that their neighbors, potential rivals, and enemies are not arming themselves with the world's ultimate weapon.

Along with the inspection and verification system provided by International Atomic Energy Agency (IAEA) safeguards, the treaty is a vital strand in a web of interlocking, overlapping, and mutually reinforcing political pledges and legal commitments. . . .

The NPT and the IAEA safeguards system are not panaceas and they are certainly not fail-safe. They do not determine decisions by countries on whether to acquire nuclear weapons. But this harsh truth overlooks the positive influence they do exert. Submitting to comprehensive IAEA safeguards and taking NPT membership are earnests of the intent not to develop nuclear weapons.

Mitchell Reiss, *The Wilson Quarterly*, Spring 1995.

Taken together, the NPT and the IAEA will help eliminate the uncertainty and fear that could turn regional rivalries into regional nuclear arms races. But we will not rest on our laurels. President Clinton intends to forge ahead with the most ambitious arms control program since the dawn of the nuclear age.

The challenges include a treaty ending nuclear testing once and for all, a ban on the production of fissile material, the agreement to stop the North Korean nuclear program in its tracks, as well as our efforts to stop the spread of chemical and biological weapons and the ballistic missiles that deliver them.

I will always remember the moment when the treaty was extended. The delegates of the world spontaneously applauded, for they knew that we had presented a gift to the next generation by forever reducing the risk that additional countries will become nuclear powers.

"Once the [Nuclear Non-Proliferation Treaty] was indefinitely extended, the non-nuclear states lost whatever leverage they had in forcing the nuclear weapons states to [disarm]."

THE NUCLEAR NON-PROLIFERATION TREATY DOES NOT FURTHER NUCLEAR DISARMAMENT

Frank Blackaby

The Nuclear Non-Proliferation Treaty (NPT), implemented in 1970, is an agreement among 186 countries that non-nuclear states will not develop nuclear weapons, while nuclear states will negotiate nuclear disarmament. In the following viewpoint, Frank Blackaby asserts that the NPT has not achieved its goal of nuclear disarmament because the nuclear powers are unwilling to relinquish their weapons. The only way to compel the nuclear states to disarm, maintains Blackaby, is for the non-nuclear states to issue a warning that they will withdraw from the treaty.

As you read, consider the following questions:

1. How have the nuclear states violated the provisions of the NPT, in Blackaby's opinion?
2. According to Blackaby, what is the current state of nuclear disarmament?
3. Why would a withdrawal warning on the part of non-nuclear states be effective, in the author's view?

Reprinted from Frank Blackaby, "Time for a Peasant Revolt," *The Bulletin of the Atomic Scientists*, November/December 1997, by permission of *The Bulletin of the Atomic Scientists*. Copyright 1997 by the Educational Foundation for Nuclear Science, 6042 S. Kimbark Ave., Chicago, IL 60637, USA. A one-year subscription is US$28.

One hundred and eighty states have ratified or acceded to the Nuclear Non-Proliferation Treaty (NPT) as non-nuclear weapon states. That treaty, which went into effect in 1968, was never intended to be an indefinite license for a two-tier world of nuclear haves and have-nots. It embodied a bargain. The majority of states would not acquire nuclear weapons. Meanwhile, the nuclear states would negotiate nuclear disarmament.

The nuclear weapon states never kept their side of the bargain. For 20 years after signing the treaty, they competed intensively in developing new nuclear weapon systems—missiles with multiple warheads, terrain-following cruise missiles, enhanced radiation weapons. They moved their nuclear weapon tests underground, but did nothing to reduce their number.

In 1995 the non-nuclear weapon states came under intense pressure, mainly from the United States, to agree to an indefinite extension of the NPT. They yielded—and got very little in exchange: a more thorough review process and a test ban that leaves the nuclear weapon states free to "modernize" their weapons.

PROLIFERATION CONTINUES

Nuclear disarmament is as distant as ever. Even if the second Strategic Arms Reduction Treaty is ratified by Russia, the United States and Russia will still retain some 20,000 nuclear warheads in the year 2007, if "hedges" and spares are included. The nuclear weapon powers have successfully sold the story that even if further nuclear disarmament does take place, it would have to be stretched out over decades. That simply is not true. With only a small investment in new facilities, the whole world stock of nuclear weapons could be dismantled in seven years.

The United States, France, Britain, and Russia have very little interest in the views of the non-nuclear weapon states. They refuse to agree to any discussion of nuclear disarmament in Geneva. The United States—supported only by Israel, a covert nuclear weapon state—has voted against convening a Special Session on Disarmament at the United Nations in the year 2000.

TIME FOR A PEASANTS' REVOLT

The United States believes that the non-nuclear weapon states are docile and disorganized. It is time for a peasants' revolt. The 180 non-nuclear states should meet and issue a warning along these lines:

The nuclear weapon states are in violation of the NPT. Given that, it is legitimate for any state, or states, to withdraw from the treaty. Non-nuclear states will therefore withdraw within two years, unless the nuclear weapon states agree in some forum to start genuine negotiations designed to ultimately rid the world of nuclear weapons.

It is an outrageous proposal. But once the NPT was indefinitely extended, the non-nuclear states lost whatever leverage they had in forcing the nuclear weapon states to live up to their end of the deal.

THE NUCLEAR NON-PROLIFERATION TREATY HAS NOT REDUCED NUCLEAR DANGER

In spite of the NPT, about 20 countries already have nuclear weapons capability—or soon will have. Either they are able to make their own weapons and have decided to hold back, or they want this capability and are not far off because they have the necessary technology.

In spite of the NPT, the use of such arms is more likely today than it ever was: Fanatics do not fear death; drug cartels have no territory to defend. And for them, the conventional principles of nuclear deterrence, which presuppose the fear of reprisals, no longer have any meaning.

In spite of the NPT, technology continues to develop, and a rudimentary nuclear weapon is now within easy reach of any group that has a few hundred million dollars to spend. This is all the more true for tomorrow's most dangerous weapon—the "radioactive" weapon—which calls only for a few hundred grams of fissile materials.

Jacques Attali, *New Perspectives Quarterly*, Summer 1995.

The withdrawal warning would have to be issued by at least 30 non-nuclear states—ideally by more than a hundred. If only a few states issued the warning, they could be picked off by punitive action.

Would the move be effective? Very possibly. A primary objective of U.S. nuclear weapons policy is to prevent further proliferation. No U.S. president wants to see the nonproliferation regime unravel before his eyes. If faced by a revolt of the peasants, the United States could hardly do nothing.

Should non-nuclear states start developing nuclear weapons? No. A decision to withdraw from the treaty if necessary would be a powerful warning signal by itself.

REJECTING THE NPT

Most non-nuclear weapon states judge their status to be in their own interest. Indeed, most are now in regional nuclear-weapon-free zones. The zone agreements should not be dismantled. My proposal is simply this: It is time to think about rejecting a U.S.-imposed treaty unless that treaty can be made to work as intended.

Is this proposal dangerous? Yes. No one wants to see the NPT crumble. But it would be even more dangerous to allow current nuclear weapon policies to persist for another 20 years without any attempt to muster effective countervailing pressure.

It is an axiom of the case for zero nuclear weapons that in the long run a two-tier world is unsustainable. We have already had a long run of that—30 years since the NPT was signed. Now is the time to try somewhat more powerful action to bring that long run to an end. This proposal could produce a fair and open warning to the nuclear weapon powers that they can no longer ignore their central obligation under the terms of the NPT.

PERIODICAL BIBLIOGRAPHY

The following articles have been selected to supplement the diverse views presented in this chapter. Addresses are provided for periodicals not indexed in the *Readers' Guide to Periodical Literature*, the *Alternative Press Index*, the *Social Sciences Index*, or the *Index to Legal Periodicals and Books*.

Madeleine Albright	"The Spread of Nuclear Arms: The Necessity of Treaties," *Vital Speeches of the Day*, June 10, 1998.
Ken Alibek	"Russia's Deadly Expertise," *New York Times*, March 27, 1998.
Jacques Attali	"Trading in the Apocalypse," *New Perspectives Quarterly*, Summer 1995.
Tom Zamora Collina and Eric Sohn	"A Ban for All Seasons," *Nucleus*, Winter 1997–98. Available from 2 Brattle Sq., Cambridge, MA 02238.
CQ Researcher	"Chemical and Biological Weapons," January 31, 1997. Available from 1414 22nd St. NW, Washington, DC 20037.
Sidney D. Drell	"Reasons to Ratify, Not to Stall," *New York Times*, June 2, 1998.
William Epstein	"Indefinite Extension—with Increased Accountability," *Bulletin of the Atomic Scientists*, July/August 1995.
Douglas J. Feith	"Chemical Reaction," *New Republic*, March 24, 1997.
Morton H. Halperin	"Let the U.S. Renounce Underground Weapons Testing and the First-Strike Option," *Insight*, November 17, 1997. Available from 3600 New York Ave. NE, Washington, DC 20002.
Richard Lugar and Joseph Biden	"An End to Chemical Weapons," *Christian Science Monitor*, February 28, 1997.
Elizabeth Olson	"Easy to Build, Hard to Detect: How to Track Biological Arms?" *Christian Science Monitor*, February 20, 1998.
James Schlesinger	"Nukes: Test Them or Lose Them," *Wall Street Journal*, November 19, 1997.
John Yoo	"The Chemical Weapons Treaty Is Unconstitutional," *Wall Street Journal*, April 16, 1997.

GLOSSARY

ABM Treaty   A 1972 treaty between the United States and the former Soviet Union that prohibits the deployment of a nationwide defense system against **ballistic missiles**.

arms control   The process of negotiations between two or more nations to limit or reduce arms. Usually refers to efforts to control **weapons of mass destruction**.

arms race   Refers to the United States and former Soviet Union's race to develop nuclear arms during the **Cold War**. *See also* **MAD**.

atomic bomb   A bomb whose energy comes from the **fission** of **uranium** or **plutonium** atoms.

ballistic missile   A missile powered on takeoff by rocket engines, but which descends to its target in a free-fall after the engines burn out.

ballistic missile defense   A defense system whose goal is to intercept foreign **ballistic missiles** before they reach their target.

bilateral   Action taken equally by two sides or nations.

biological weapons   A bacteria or virus that is released intentionally to inflict harm. Potential biological weapons include anthrax bacteria, the smallpox virus, and the plague virus.

bio-terrorism   Acts of terrorism committed using **biological weapons**.

chemical weapon   A chemical substance that causes death or severe physical harm through inhalation or exposure to the skin. The most common chemical weapons are sarin, VX, and mustard gasses.

civil defense   Measures taken by civilians—such as building shelters and stockpiling food—in preparation for natural disasters, acts of terrorism, or war.

Cold War   A period of East-West competition, tension, and conflict that fell short of a full-scale war. The war, which began with the end of World War II in 1945 and lasted until the late 1980s, incited an **arms race** between the United States and the former Soviet Union. *See also* **MAD**.

de-alert   To increase the amount of time needed to launch a nuclear weapon.

deterrence   The threat of nuclear retaliation that keeps a nation from launching a **first strike**.

DOD   Department of Defense.

DOE   Department of Energy.

downwinders   Refers to residents who have been exposed to radioactive fallout from the nuclear testing activities conducted at the Nevada Test Site.

Duma   The Russian congress.

export controls   Measures aimed at controlling the exporting of materials, equipment, and technology that can be used to construct weapons of mass destruction.

first strike   An attempt to gain a military advantage by launching a nuclear attack against an opponent's nuclear arsenal before the opponent can launch its weapons.

fission   The process by which a neutron strikes the nucleus of an atom and splits it into fragments, releasing heat and radiation.

fusion   The formation of a heavier nucleus of an atom from two lighter nuclei, with an attendant release of energy.

IAEA   International Atomic Energy Agency. An organization affiliated with the United Nations that oversees many nations' civilian nuclear programs and that monitors the **NPT**.

ICBM   Intercontinental **ballistic missile**. A long-range **ballistic missile** capable of reaching targets on the other side of the globe.

INF   Intermediate-range nuclear forces. **Tactical nuclear weapons** with a range between three hundred and thirty-four hundred miles.

INF Treaty   A 1988 treaty between the United States and the former Soviet Union eliminating all **INF** missiles.

kiloton   The explosive power equivalent to one thousand tons of TNT.

MAD   An acronym for mutually assured destruction, this term refers to the Cold War philosophy that an actual war between the United States and the former Soviet Union would not take place since each possessed the nuclear capacity to destroy the other.

megaton   The explosive power equivalent to one million tons of TNT.

NATO   North Atlantic Treaty Organization. A military alliance among the United States, Canada, and many European nations.

NPT   Nuclear Non-Proliferation Treaty. A treaty first signed in 1968 by nations that promised not to spread or acquire nuclear arms.

plutonium   A highly toxic and radioactive element produced by nuclear reactors and usually used for the **weapons-grade material** of nuclear weapons.

preemptive   *See* **first strike**.

proliferation   The continued increase in the number of nuclear weapons. Horizontal proliferation refers to the spread of nuclear weapons to other nations while vertical proliferation refers to the upgrading of nuclear weapons technology within the arsenals of acknowledged nuclear weapons states.

ratification The process by which a legislature formally approves a treaty.

START Strategic Arms Reduction Treaty signed in 1991 by the United States and the former Soviet Union that drastically reduced certain classes of **ballistic missiles**.

START II The second Strategic Arms Reduction Treaty, signed in 1993 by the United States and Russia. Both parties agree to reduce their **strategic nuclear weapons** to no more than 3,000 to 3,500 by 2007. The treaty, ratified by the U.S. Senate in 1995, is still awaiting **ratification** by the Russian **Duma**.

START III The third Strategic Arms Reduction Treaty, developed by U.S. President Bill Clinton and Russian President Boris Yeltsin in March 1997. It aims to reduce both countries' **strategic nuclear weapons** to no more than 2,000 to 2,500 by 2007. Negotiations are still taking place on this treaty.

Star Wars The popular name for the Strategic Defense Initiative, a defense plan proposed by President Ronald Reagan in 1983 that calls for a space-based shield against foreign **ballistic missiles**.

Strategic Defense Initiative *See* **Star Wars**.

strategic nuclear weapons Nuclear weapons with the range to reach deep inside the opponent's territory and destroy strategically important targets.

tactical nuclear weapons Short-range nuclear weapons that can only be used in nearby battlefields.

toxin weapons Poisons that are produced by living organisms. *See also* **biological weapons**.

unilateral Action taken by only one side or nation.

uranium A radioactive element found in natural ores and used in the manufacturing of nuclear weapons.

verification The process of confirming compliance with arms control treaties through satellite monitoring or on-site inspections.

warhead The device in missiles containing the nuclear explosive. The term "bomb" is usually reserved for gravity bombs dropped from the air.

weapons-grade material The type of **plutonium** or **uranium** most suitable for nuclear weapons.

weapons of mass destruction Biological, chemical, and nuclear weapons capable of causing widespread damage.

yield The explosive power of nuclear weapons measured in the equivalent amount of TNT.

zero yield A nuclear detonation that yields no explosive power.

CHRONOLOGY OF BIOLOGICAL AND CHEMICAL WEAPONS

1346	Crimean Tartars hurl plague-infected corpses over the city walls of Kaffa, where their enemies lived.
1797	Napoleon attempts to infect the inhabitants of the besieged city of Mantua with swamp fever.
1800s	American settlers deliberately give Native Americans blankets infected with smallpox, which causes widespread epidemics.
1907	The Hague Convention outlaws chemical weapons. The U.S. does not sign the treaty.
1925	The Geneva Protocol, an international treaty banning biological warfare, is signed.
1935	Italy uses mustard gas in its conquest of Abyssinia (Ethiopia).
1936	Japan uses chemical weapons during its invasion of China. German chemical laboratories produce the first nerve agent, Tabun.
1945	Germans use Zyklon-B in the extermination of Jews.
1947	President Harry Truman withdraws the Geneva Protocol from Senate consideration.
1961	The Kennedy administration increases the funding of U.S. chemical weapons programs.
1962	Chemical weapons are loaded on U.S. planes during the Cuban missile crisis.
1969	President Richard Nixon declares a U.S. moratorium on chemical weapons production and biological weapons possession.
1972	The Biological and Toxin Weapons Convention, an international treaty banning the possession of biological weapons, is signed. Members of the U.S. fascist group Order of the Rising Sun are arrested for the possession of 30 to 40 kilograms of typhoid bacteria cultures, which they planned to disseminate in the water supplies of Midwestern cities.
1982	A man is reportedly arrested for preparing to poison the Los Angeles water system with a biological agent.
1983	Two brothers are arrested by the FBI for manufacturing an ounce of ricin.
1986	In an attempt to influence an Oregon election, members of the Bhagwan Shree Rajneesh sect poison salad bars with salmonella; 750 become ill.

1988	Iran-Iraq War ends. Shortly after, evidence emerges that Iraq used chemical weapons on Iranian soldiers and civilians, as well as on members of the Kurdish ethnic minority within its own borders.
1990	The U.S. and the former Soviet Union pledge to reduce chemical weapons stockpiles by 2002. Iraq threatens to use chemical weapons on Israel.
1991	The United States and coalition forces bomb at least 28 alleged biological and chemical production sites in Iraq during the Gulf War.
1992	Gulf War veterans report the development of post-war health problems involving a variety of symptoms; these health problems, collectively referred to as Gulf War Syndrome, are thought to be the result of exposure to Iraq's chemical weapons. In Germany, police thwart a neo-Nazi attempt to release cyanide in a synagogue.
1993	President Bill Clinton continues to bomb Iraqi biological and chemical weapons facilities; UN inspectors begin a program to dismantle Iraqi weapons. The U.S. signs the Chemical Weapons Convention, a treaty barring the use, production, and transfer of chemical weapons for any purpose; treaty members pledge to destroy their chemical weapons stockpiles by 2007.
1994	Apocalyptic cult Aum Shinrikyo releases the nerve agent sarin in Matsumoto, Japan; 8 people die and 200 are hospitalized.
1995	
March	Aum Shinrikyo launches a sarin nerve gas attack on the Tokyo subway system; 12 people die and 5,500 people are affected. Two members of the Minnesota Patriots Council, an antitax group, are convicted for planning to use ricin to assassinate government officials.
April	The FBI thwarts a possible sarin gas attack at Disneyland.
May	A member of the Aryan Nation is arrested for ordering plague bacteria.
December	An Arkansas man is arrested for the possession of 130 grams of ricin.
1997	Two chlorine bombs are activated in crowded shopping malls in Australia. The U.S. ratifies the Chemical Weapons Convention in April.
1998	Two men are arrested in Las Vegas for the possession of anthrax, a deadly bacteria. The charges are dropped when officials learn that the substance is actually an anthrax vaccine.

CHRONOLOGY OF NUCLEAR WEAPONS

1942

August 13 · U.S. Army Corps of Engineers establishes the Manhattan Project to develop an atomic bomb.

1945

July 16 · The United States tests the first atomic bomb at Alamogordo, New Mexico.

August 6 · The United States drops the first uranium bomb on Hiroshima, Japan.

August 9 · The United States drops the first plutonium bomb on Nagasaki, Japan.

August 29 · First Soviet atomic bomb exploded.

1946 · The United States proposes the Baruch Plan, which would prevent nuclear proliferation by placing all nuclear materials and technology under international control. The Soviet Union rejects the plan.

1949 · The Soviet Union begins testing nuclear weapons.

1950

January 31 · President Truman directs the Atomic Energy Commission to develop a hydrogen bomb and tactical nuclear weapons.

1952

October 3 · Great Britain begins testing nuclear weapons.

1953

March · Americans Julius and Ethel Rosenberg executed after being found guilty of stealing U.S. nuclear secrets and passing them to the Soviet Union.

1957 · International Atomic Energy Agency (IAEA) is founded under the auspices of the United Nations to help nations develop peaceful nuclear programs. Careful monitoring ensures that materials are not diverted for nuclear weapons.

1958

October 31 · Nuclear test ban negotiations among the United States, Great Britain, and the Soviet Union start in Geneva, Switzerland, and officials from those countries announce a test moratorium.

1960

February 13 · France tests a nuclear weapon in the Sahara Desert.

1961

September · The United States resumes limited underground nuclear testing.

1962

October 22–28 · Cuban missile crisis. The United States imposes a naval blockade on Cuba because of the placement of Soviet nuclear missiles there. After a declaration to defend its rights, the Soviet Union finally relents and removes the missiles.

1963

October 10 — Partial Test Ban Treaty is ratified by the United States, Great Britain, and the Soviet Union, prohibiting nuclear testing in the atmosphere, in space, or under water.

1964 — China begins testing nuclear weapons.

1965 — Multilateral negotiations begin on a formal treaty to prevent the spread of nuclear weapons.

1967–68 — U.S. inventory of nuclear weapons reaches a peak of about thirty-two thousand weapons.

1968

April 22 — Treaty for the Prohibition of Nuclear Weapons in Latin America (also known as the Treaty of Tlatelolco) takes effect.

June — The United States, the Soviet Union, Great Britain, and fifty-nine other countries sign the Nuclear Non-Proliferation Treaty (NPT).

1970

March 5 — Nuclear Non-Proliferation Treaty is ratified.

1971 — Anti-Ballistic Missile (ABM) Treaty limits the United States to two hundred nuclear interceptors.

1972

May — Strategic Arms Limitations Talks (SALT I) agreements signed by the United States and the Soviet Union.

November — Negotiations begin on SALT II, a long-term treaty on strategic nuclear weapons.

1974 — India tests a nuclear bomb but claims that the test is for peaceful purposes.

July 3 — The United States and the Soviet Union sign the Threshold Test Ban Treaty, limiting nuclear tests to 150 kilotons.

1978 — Congress passes the Nuclear Nonproliferation Act, requiring tighter restrictions on the sale and the use of plutonium.

1979

June 18 — President Carter and General Secretary Brezhnev sign the SALT II Treaty, limiting the number of nuclear weapons in the United States and the Soviet Union.

September 2 — A U.S. satellite detects an apparent South African-Israeli nuclear test off the South African coast.

1981

June 7 — Israeli jets destroy Iraq's Osirak nuclear research reactor.

1982 — U.S. nuclear weapons inventory reduced to about twenty-four thousand weapons, of which about half are strategic and half tactical.

June 29 — Strategic Arms Reduction Talks (START) begin in Geneva, Switzerland.

1985

Australia, New Zealand, and nine other nations sign the South Pacific Nuclear-Free Zone Treaty (also known as the Treaty of Rarotonga).

1987

December 8

President Reagan and Soviet general secretary Gorbachev sign the Intermediate-Range Nuclear Forces (INF) Treaty, eliminating short- and intermediate-range nuclear weapons.

1990

February 8

A Soviet KGB report concludes that North Korea "continues scientific and design-testing work leading toward making nuclear weapons."

March 20

British agents in London intercept a shipment of capacitors used to trigger atomic bombs. The devices were bound for Iraq.

July 15

Iraq's ambassador to the United States, Mohamed al-Mashat, says in a newspaper interview that "there is no plan to develop nuclear weapons in Iraq."

1991

April 3

U.N. Security Council passes Resolution 687, ending the Persian Gulf War, and orders the destruction or removal of all of Iraq's prohibited nuclear material and facilities.

May 6 and 12

The United States and the Soviet Union destroy their last remaining intermediate-range missiles in compliance with the INF Treaty.

May 14–22

The IAEA's initial inspection in Iraq following the Persian Gulf War discovers that Iraq has produced small quantities of plutonium.

July 9

South Africa signs the Nuclear Non-Proliferation Treaty (NPT).

July 31

George Bush and Mikhail Gorbachev sign the START Treaty, the first accord requiring reductions in strategic warheads.

September

Pakistani prime minister Benazir Bhutto announces that her country has the capability to produce a nuclear weapon.

September 27

President Bush announces a major disarmament initiative: the removal of ground-launched nuclear weapons from Europe and of all nuclear weapons from South Korea, ending ground alert for nuclear-armed bombers, and accelerating the elimination of strategic nuclear weapons covered by START.

October 5

Soviets respond to the U.S. initiative with a similar initiative: the removal of all tactical nuclear weapons from ships and submarines; reductions to five thousand accountable warheads, one thousand less than agreed to under START; and the destruction of all nuclear artillery projectiles, nuclear land mines, and nuclear warheads for nonstrategic missiles.

October 11–21	IAEA inspectors find traces of weapons-grade uranium at Iraq's Tuwaitha nuclear research center.
October 17	NATO decides to eliminate 80 percent of its nuclear weapons—leaving only seven hundred air-delivered atomic bombs at European bases.
December 13	Argentina and Brazil agree to place all of their nuclear facilities and materials under IAEA safeguards.

1992

January 28	In his State of the Union Address, President Bush announces the cancellation of the Midgetman missile program and an end to advanced cruise missile and Trident II submarine missile warhead production.
January 29	Russian president Boris Yeltsin announces a halt in production of all long-range nuclear air- and sea-launched cruise missiles.
January 30	North Korea signs an agreement with the IAEA—six years after signing the NPT—allowing inspection and monitoring of all its nuclear facilities and activities.
March 9	China signs the Nuclear Non-Proliferation Treaty.
April 3	Members of the twenty-seven nation Nuclear Suppliers Group agree to voluntary international rules limiting the sale of machinery and materials that can be used to build a nuclear weapon.
May 11–16	IAEA director Hans Blix tours several of North Korea's nuclear facilities.
May 22	China sets off its largest ever underground nuclear test. The explosion is estimated to be in the one-megaton range.
May 23	Russia, the Ukraine, Belarus, and Kazakhstan agree to abide by the START treaty signed by the now-defunct Soviet Union.
June 16	The United States and Russia sign an agreement reducing both of their nuclear arsenals to thirty-five hundred strategic weapons each.
June 19	France signs the Nuclear Non-Proliferation Treaty.
July 2	President Bush announces that the United States has completed its withdrawal of all tactical land- and sea-based nuclear weapons outside the country.

1993

January	Presidents Boris Yeltsin and George Bush sign new Strategic Arms Reduction Treaty (START II) which spells the end for almost two-thirds of U.S. and Russian nuclear missiles.
March	South Africa acknowledges for the first time that it had made nuclear bombs but says all six were dismantled by 1991.

1994

February	United States and Russia agree to stop targeting strategic nuclear weapons at each other's territories.

| October | United States and North Korea reach nuclear accord under which Pyongyang would switch to safer technology, amid fears that it had been trying to develop nuclear weapons secretly. |

1995

May 11	World nations agree to make permanent the 25-year-old Non-Proliferation Treaty (NPT).
May 15	China conducts an underground nuclear test just days after the successful extension of the NPT treaty.
June 13	President Jacques Chirac announces France will resume nuclear weapons testing at its South Pacific site in September, setting off widespread protests throughout the area.
August 6	Hiroshima commemorates the 50th anniversary of atomic bombing.
September 5	France conducts an underground nuclear test on Mururoa Atoll, bringing worldwide condemnation and rioting in Tahiti.

1996

January 27	France conducts its sixth and final nuclear test.
March 25	France, Britain, and the United States sign the South Pacific Nuclear-Free Zone Treaty.
April 11	Forty-three African states sign a treaty declaring Africa free of nuclear weapons.
June 8	China carries out a nuclear explosion at the Lop Nor test site in Xinjiang.

1997

| July 2 | United States begins a round of controversial underground nuclear weapons-related tests in the Nevada desert. |
| September 18 | The United States conducts a second underground explosive test on radioactive plutonium at a Nevada site. |

1998

February 24	France's National Assembly votes unanimously to ratify a global treaty banning nuclear weapons tests.
March 19	The U.S. Department of Energy announces that it will begin a series of underground explosive tests on radioactive plutonium later in the month.
May 11	India conducts three underground nuclear tests in the western desert state of Rajasthan.
May 13	India conducts two more tests.
May 28	Pakistan conducts five successful nuclear tests in response to the same number of tests by its regional arch-rival, India.
May 30	Pakistan conducts another nuclear test, saying it completes the current series.

FOR FURTHER DISCUSSION

CHAPTER 1

1. Marie Isabelle Chevrier argues that the threat of chemical or biological terrorism is exaggerated. What reasons does she provide for why terrorists will not be inclined to use weapons of mass destruction? Do you find her argument persuasive? Explain your answer.

2. John Leifer maintains that the disintegration of the Soviet Union has greatly increased the risk of nuclear terrorism. Karl Heinz Kamp disagrees. Whose evidence do you find more convincing? Why?

CHAPTER 2

1. This chapter presents three different perspectives on U.S. nuclear disarmament: Robert G. Spulak Jr. contends that the United States should retain a strong nuclear arsenal; William F. Burns argues that the U.S. should reduce its stockpile of nuclear weapons; and Lee Butler and Joseph Rotblat maintain that nuclear weapons should be eliminated entirely. What are the benefits and dangers of each policy?

2. Robert G. Spulak Jr. believes that nuclear weapons serve the important purpose of deterring war. Lee Butler and Joseph Rotblat, in contrast, allege that nuclear weapons are inherently dangerous. Which view do you find more convincing? Why?

3. Removing nuclear weapons from alert status would increase the amount of time needed to launch a weapon. Tim Zimmermann argues that de-alerting nuclear weapons would reduce the likelihood of a nuclear attack. How does he support his view?

CHAPTER 3

1. The authors of this chapter provide different suggestions for how the United States can defend itself from attacks involving weapons of mass destruction. Of their proposals, which do you feel is most essential? Which is least essential? Why?

2. Curt Weldon contends that the United States needs a defense against ballistic missiles. Lisbeth Gronlund and David Wright argue that such a defense is unnecessary. How do these authors' differing views on the likelihood of a nuclear attack influence their opinions on ballistic missile defenses? Based on what you have read in the other chapters of this book, do you feel that a nuclear attack is likely enough to warrant the construction of a missile defense?

3. Based on the viewpoints of Frank J. Cilluffo, Jack Thomas Tomarchio, and Richard Preston, do you think the United States is prepared for a chemical or biological attack? Why or why not? Can you think of other ways the U.S. could prepare for such an attack?

CHAPTER 4

1. The main controversy surrounding bans against weapons of mass destruction is whether such bans can be enforced. What enforcement methods do the authors in this chapter suggest? In your opinion, are weapons bans worthwhile even if they cannot be enforced? Why or why not?

2. The stated goal of the Nuclear Non-Proliferation Treaty is to prevent non-nuclear countries from developing nuclear weapons while current nuclear powers negotiate disarmament. Madeleine K. Albright believes that the treaty's indefinite extension is a positive step toward nuclear disarmament. Frank Blackaby disagrees. What reasons do they provide for their views?

ORGANIZATIONS TO CONTACT

The editors have compiled the following list of organizations concerned with the issues debated in this book. The descriptions are derived from materials provided by the organizations. All have publications or information available for interested readers. The list was compiled on the date of publication of the present volume; the information provided here may change. Be aware that many organizations take several weeks or longer to respond to inquiries, so allow as much time as possible.

The American Civil Defense Association (TACDA)
PO Box 1057, Starke, FL 32091
(800) 425-5397 • (904) 964-5397 • fax: (904) 964-9641
e-mail: defense@tacda.org • website: http://www.tacda.org

TACDA was established in the early 1960s in an effort to help promote civil defense awareness and disaster preparedness, both in the military and private sector, and to assist citizens in their efforts to prepare for all types of natural and man-made disasters. Publications include the quarterly *Journal of Civil Defense* and the *TACDA Alert* newsletter.

America's Future
7800 Bonhomme Ave., St. Louis, MO 63105
(314) 725-6003 • fax: (314) 721-3373
e-mail: info@americasfuture.net
website: http://www.americasfuture.net

America's Future seeks to educate the public about the importance of the principles upon which the U.S. government is founded and on the value of the free enterprise system. It supports continued U.S. testing of nuclear weapons and their usefulness as a deterrent of war. The group publishes the monthly newsletter *America's Future*.

Arms Control Association (ACA)
1726 M St. NW, Suite 201, Washington, DC 20036
(202) 463-8270 • fax: (202) 463-8273
e-mail: aca@armscontrol.org • website: http://www.armscontrol.org

The Arms Control Association is a nonprofit organization dedicated to promoting public understanding of and support for effective arms control policies. ACA seeks to increase public appreciation of the need to limit arms, reduce international tensions, and promote world peace. It publishes the monthly magazine *Arms Control Today*.

Barksdale Air Force Base
website: http://www.barksdale.af.mil/htmls/bafb.html

This site is an excellent example of a nuclear base's home page and includes a phone book, photos, and organization diagrams.

Carnegie Endowment for International Peace

1779 Massachusetts Ave. NW, Washington, DC 20036
(202) 483-7600 • fax: (202) 483-1840
e-mail: info@ceip.org • website: http://www.ceip.org

The Carnegie Endowment for International Peace conducts research on international affairs and U.S. foreign policy. Issues concerning nuclear weapons and proliferation are often discussed in articles published in its quarterly journal *Foreign Policy*.

Center for Defense Information (CDI)

1779 Massachusetts Ave. NW, Suite 615, Washington, DC 20036
(202) 332-0600 • fax: (202) 462-4559
e-mail: info@cdi.org • website: http://www.cdi.org

CDI is comprised of civilians and former military officers who oppose both excessive expenditures for weapons and policies that increase the danger of war. The center serves as an independent monitor of the military, analyzing spending, policies, weapon systems, and related military issues. It publishes the *Defense Monitor* ten times per year.

Center for Nonproliferation Studies

Monterey Institute for International Studies
425 Van Buren St., Monterey, CA 93940
(831) 647-4154 • fax: (831) 647-3519
website: http://cns.miis.edu

The center researches all aspects of nonproliferation and works to combat the spread of weapons of mass destruction. The center produces research databases and has multiple reports, papers, speeches, and congressional testimony available on-line. Its main publication is *The Nonproliferation Review*, which is published three times per year.

Chemical and Biological Arms Control Institute

2111 Eisenhower Ave., Suite 302, Alexandria, VA 22314
(703) 739-1538 • fax: (703) 739-1525
e-mail: cbaci@cbaci.org • website: http://www.cbaci.org

The institute is a nonprofit corporation that supports arms control and nonproliferation, particularly of chemical and biological weapons. In addition to conducting research, the institute plans meetings and seminars and assists in the implementation of weapons-control treaties. Its publications include *The Dispatch*, published bimonthly, and numerous fact sheets, monographs, and reports.

Henry L. Stimson Center

11 Dupont Circle NW, 9th Fl., Washington, DC 20036
(202) 223-5956 • fax: (202) 238-9604
website: http://www.stimson.org

The Stimson Center is an independent, nonprofit public policy institute committed to finding and promoting innovative solutions to the security challenges confronting the United States and other nations. The center directs the Chemical and Biological Weapons Nonproliferation Project, which serves as a clearinghouse of information related to the monitoring and implementation of the 1993 Chemical Weapons Convention. The center produces occasional papers, reports, handbooks, and books on chemical and biological weapon policy, nuclear policy, and eliminating weapons of mass destruction.

Peace Action
1819 H St. NW, Suite 425, Washington, DC 20006
(202) 862-9740 • fax: (202) 862-9762
e-mail: paprog@igc.org • website: http://www.peace-action.org

Peace Action is a grassroots peace and justice organization that works for policy changes in Congress and the United Nations, as well as state and city legislatures. The national office houses an Organizing Department that promotes education and activism on topics related to peace and disarmament issues. The organization produces a quarterly newsletter and also publishes an annual voting record for members of Congress.

Union of Concerned Scientists (UCS)
2 Brattle Sq., Cambridge, MA 02238
(617) 547-5552 • fax: (617) 864-9405
e-mail: ucs@ucsusa.org • website: http://www.ucsusa.org

UCS is concerned about the impact of advanced technology on society. It supports nuclear arms control as a means to reduce nuclear weapons. Publications include the quarterly *Nucleus* newsletter and reports and briefs concerning nuclear proliferation.

United States Arms Control and Disarmament Agency (ACDA)
320 21st St. NW, Washington, DC 20451
(800) 581-ACDA • fax: (202) 647-6928
website: http://www.acda.gov

The mission of the agency is to strengthen the national security of the United States by formulating, advocating, negotiating, implementing, and verifying effective arms control, nonproliferation, and disarmament policies, strategies, and agreements. In so doing, ACDA ensures that arms control is fully integrated into the development and conduct of U.S. national security policy. The agency publishes fact sheets on the disarmament of weapons of mass destruction as well as on-line records of speeches, treaties, and reports related to arms control.

Washington File
U.S. Information Agency
301 Fourth St. SW, Room 602, Washington, DC 20547
(202) 619-4355
e-mail: inquiry@usia.gov
website: http://www.usia.gov/products/washfile.htm

This site is the best single source of current releases and government information relating to foreign affairs. It is maintained by the U.S. Information Agency, an independent foreign affairs agency within the executive branch of the U.S. government.

BIBLIOGRAPHY OF BOOKS

Graham T. Allison — *Avoiding Nuclear Anarchy: Containing the Threat of Loose Russian Nuclear Weapons and Fissile Material.* Cambridge, MA: MIT Press, 1996.

Gar Alperovitz — *The Decision to Use the Atomic Bomb and the Architecture of an American Myth.* New York: Knopf, 1995.

Eric Arnett, ed. — *Nuclear Weapons After the Comprehensive Test Ban: Implications for Modernization and Proliferation.* New York: Oxford University Press, 1996.

Timothy J. Botti — *Ace in the Hole: Why the United States Did Not Use Nuclear Weapons in the Cold War, 1945 to 1965.* Westport, CT: Greenwood Press, 1996.

Paul S. Boyer — *Fallout: A Historian Reflects on America's Half-Century Encounter with Nuclear Weapons.* Columbus: Ohio State University Press, 1998.

William E. Burrows — *Critical Mass: The Dangerous Race for Superweapons in a Fragmenting World.* New York: Simon and Schuster, 1994.

W. Seth Carus — *The Threat of Bioterrorism.* Washington, DC: National Defense University, Institute for National Strategic Studies, 1997.

Leonard A. Cole — *The Eleventh Plague: The Politics of Biological and Chemical Warfare.* New York: W.H. Freeman, 1997.

Malcolm Dando — *Biological Warfare in the 21st Century: Biotechnology and the Proliferation of Biological Weapons.* New York: Macmillan, 1994.

Marco De Andreis — *The Soviet Nuclear Weapon Legacy.* New York: Oxford University Press, 1995.

Randall Forsberg et al. — *Nonproliferation Primer: Preventing the Spread of Nuclear, Chemical, and Biological Weapons.* Cambridge, MA: MIT Press, 1995.

John Glenn et al. — *The U.S. Senate and the Chemical Weapons Convention: The Price of Inaction.* Washington, DC: Henry L. Stimson Center, 1995.

Sheldon H. Harris — *Factories of Death: Japanese Biological Warfare, 1932–45, and the American Cover-Up.* New York: Routledge, 1994.

Douglas Holdstock and Frank Barnaby, eds. — *Hiroshima and Nagasaki: Retrospect and Prospect.* Portland, OR: Frank Cass, 1995.

Stuart E. Johnson, ed. — *The Niche Threat: Deterring the Use of Chemical and Biological Weapons.* Washington, DC: National Defense University, 1997.

Daniel H. Jones	*Implementing the Chemical Weapons Convention.* Santa Monica, CA: RAND, 1995.
Michael Klare	*Rogue States and Nuclear Outlaws.* New York: Hill and Wang, 1995.
David A. Koplow	*Testing a Nuclear Test Ban: What Should Be Prohibited by a "Comprehensive" Treaty?* Brookfield, VT: Dartmouth, 1996.
Robert Jay Lifton and Greg Mitchell	*Hiroshima in America: Fifty Years of Denial.* New York: Putnam's Sons, 1995.
Michael J. Mazarr, ed.	*Nuclear Weapons in a Transformed World: The Challenge of Virtual Nuclear Arsenals.* New York: St. Martin's Press, 1997.
Richard M. Price	*The Chemical Weapons Taboo.* Ithaca, NY: Cornell University Press, 1997.
Mitchell Reiss	*Bridled Ambition: Why Countries Constrain Their Nuclear Capabilities.* Washington, DC: Woodrow Wilson Center Press, 1995.
Richard Rhodes	*Dark Sun: The Making of the Hydrogen Bomb.* New York: Simon and Schuster, 1995.
Brad Roberts, ed.	*Ratifying the Chemical Weapons Convention.* Washington, DC: Center for Strategic and International Studies, 1994.
Scott Douglas Sagan	*The Spread of Nuclear Weapons: A Debate.* New York: W.W. Norton, 1995.
Jonathan Schell	*The Gift of Time: The Case for Abolishing Nuclear Weapons Now.* New York: Holt, 1998.
Nancy Turtle Schulte, ed.	*Dismantlement and Destruction of Chemical, Nuclear, and Conventional Weapons.* Boston: Kluwer Academic, 1997.
Stephen I. Schwartz, ed.	*Atomic Audit: The Costs and Consequences of U.S. Nuclear Weapons Since 1940.* Washington, DC: Brookings Institution Press, 1998.
Glenn E. Schweitzer with Carole C. Dorsch	*Superterrorism: Assassins, Mobsters, and Weapons of Mass Destruction.* New York: Plenum Press, 1998.
John M. Shields and William C. Potter, eds.	*Dismantling the Cold War.* Cambridge, MA: MIT Press, 1997.
Jo Ann Shroyer	*Secret Mesa: Inside Los Alamos National Laboratory.* New York: Wiley, 1998.
Ronald T. Takaki	*Hiroshima: Why America Dropped the Atomic Bomb.* Boston: Little, Brown, 1995.

INDEX